ALLEN TATE AND THE CATHOLIC REVIVAL

ISAAC HECKER STUDIES
IN RELIGION AND AMERICAN CULTURE

ALLEN TATE AND THE CATHOLIC REVIVAL

Trace of the Fugitive Gods

Peter A. Huff

Paulist Press
New York / Mahwah, N.J.

Cover design by Kathy McKeen.

Cover photo courtesy of Princeton University Libraries.
Used with permission of Princeton University Libraries.

The Publisher thanks Mrs. Helen Tate for her gracious permission to cite selections from the letters and papers of Allen Tate in this volume. In addition, the Publisher gratefully acknowledges use of the following materials. Excerpts from the Caroline Gordon Papers and the Allen Tate Papers, Manuscripts Division, Department of Rare Books and Special Collections, Princeton University Libraries. Published with permission of Princeton University Libraries. Excerpts from the Andrew Nelson Lytle Papers and the Donald Davidson Papers, Special Collections, University Archives, Vanderbilt University. Published with permission of Vanderbilt University. Excerpts from the Radcliffe Squires Papers, Washington University Libraries, St. Louis, Missouri. Published with permission of Washington University Libraries.

Library of Congress Cataloging-in-Publication Data

Huff, Peter A.
   Allen Tate and the Catholic revival / trace of the fugitive gods / by Peter A. Huff.
     p. cm. — (Isaac Hecker studies)
   Includes bibliographical references and index.
   ISBN 0-8091-3661-9 (alk. paper)
   1. Tate, Allen, 1899–1979—Knowledge—Literature. 2. American literature—20th century—History and criticism—Theory, etc. 3. Catholics—United States—Intellectual life—History—20th century. 4. Christianity and literature—United States—History—20th century. 5. Criticism—Southern States—History—20th century. 6. Southern States—Intellectual life—1865– 7. Modernism (Literature)—Southern States. 8. Man (Christian theology) in literature. 9. Catholic converts—Southern States. 10. Tate, Allen, 1899–1979—Religion. I. Title. II. Series: Isaac Hecker studies in religion and Amerian culture.
PS3539.A74Z68   1996
818'.5209—dc20   96-12353
                                                       CIP

Published by Paulist Press
997 Macarthur Boulevard
Mahwah, New Jersey 07430

Printed and bound in the
United States of America

Contents

Dedication

To My Parents, Walter and Jane Huff

Here it was that I first found that my wandering
feet were in some beaten track.
–G. K. Chesterton

Foreword

Peter Huff's study of Allen Tate is a wonderful weaving of interconnected narratives in the history of mid-twentieth-century American Catholicism. It offers an engaging story of how a gifted writer sought to merge the Catholic literary renaissance with Southern Agrarianism and the Neo-Thomist revival in an effort to subdue the corrosive forces of modernity. But it is also the tale of a convert whose grand cultural vision for his new church would never be realized. Allen Tate's conversion to the Roman Catholic Church, like that of his contemporary Dorothy Day, was an effort to retrieve a sense of medieval cohesiveness in a modern American culture given to splintered individualism. At the time, however, most other Catholics in the United States were moving in exactly the opposite direction, trying to overcome the long-standing mistrust of their neighbors by becoming as modern and American as possible.

How does a convert to a faith rooted in authoritative and communal tradition respond to a culture given to rationalistic individualism? Often with chutzpah, as Peter Huff explains. In the 1920s and 1930s Allen Tate was a member of a group of writers at Vanderbilt University known as the Fugitive Agrarians. Many of them lamented, among other things, the ascendancy in contemporary thought of a "God without Thunder." The God of classic Christianity, they complained, had been so beaten into submission by the powers of modernity that the highest compliment one might pay to such a God was that a few scientists and philosophers still deigned to believe in him. By contrast, the Agrarians worked against the stream, challenging the canons of modern criticism in proclaiming a thunderous God no longer housebroken by the polite sensitivities of their age.

Allen Tate would go on to champion the unpopular values of Fundamentalism and the High Middle Ages, the Old South and the New Criticism. He employed everything at his disposal to stanch the wounds that beset his culture, seeking an antidote to the spiritual aridity of modern liberal thought as he saw it.

All of this occurred in the period before Vatican II, in an era of

American Catholicism too often dismissed as an intellectual dark ages marked by a narrow "siege mentality." Peter Huff shows that this was anything but the case. If the impulse of postconciliar Catholicism has been largely ecumenical and culture-affirming, ratifying notions of democratic individualism and accommodating itself to modernity, the Catholic Revival in the preconciliar period was distinctly countercultural, trying to recover the riches of the "Great Tradition." Tate and his colleagues reacted to "the vaporization of religion" in a culture cut loose from its moorings. The countercultural energy of a vibrant Catholicism was what allowed Virgil Michel, Dorothy Day, and Allen Tate all to address, in different ways, the social fragmentation of American culture. they pointed their dislocated society to an untamed God of supernatural power made accessible in the concrete, sacramental life of the church.

John Updike, in his novel *A Month of Sundays*, has similarly bemoaned the domestication of God within a Christianity held captive by its culture. Updike speaks of liberal Protestantism's "limp-wristed theology, a perfectly custardly confection of Jungian-Reichian soma-mysticism swimming in a soupy caramel of Tillichic, Jasperian, Bultmannish blather, all served up in a dime-store dish of [this] gutless generation's give-away *Gemutlichkeit*. He wants nothing of religion made amenable to the passing whims of modern culture. "Let us have it in its original stony jars or not at all!" he insists.

What makes Peter Huff's analysis of Allen Tate and the Catholic Revival of particular interest to Protestant and other non-Catholic readers is the extent to which a similar recovery of Christianity's countercultural power is sought today among writers like Stanley Hauerwas and George Lindbeck. These postmodern theologians share certain common concerns with Tate and premodern stance of the Catholic Revival. All of them have been outspokenly antimodern in their critique of liberal confidence in reason and progress, the power of the nation-state and profit economics, and the loss of Christianity's exclusivity in the name of an ever-expanding secular pluralism.

They uphold a conception of the church, as in Lindbeck's words a "small, strongly deviant minority, unsupported by cultural convention and prestige." Whereas Lindbeck and Hauerwas, after Rahner, define this "Church of the diaspora" as similar to the pre-Constantinian experience of the early church, Tate and his colleagues sought its reality in recovering the last remnant of a Southern medieval Thomism. In either case, they would urge Christians to redefine themselves as a colony of "resident aliens" in a foreign world. Theological discourse would assume for them the role of "dispatches from the front," to borrow a recent phrase from Hauerwas.

Tate and his postmodern cousins further share a conviction that religion, far from being a privatized affair, is more characteristic of a culture with its own language and grammar. It isn't so much "a set of propositions to be believed," says Lindbeck, as "the medium in which one moves, a set of skills that one employs in living one's life." To imagine religion as purely a matter of individual experience and expression, disconnected from its cultural-linguistic matrix, is impossible. As Hauerwas argues, "There is simply no place to start thinking prior to being engaged in a tradition."

In each of these ways, Tate is able to prefigure a postmodern reading of the church vis-à-vis its culture. The important difference between the two perspectives is that Tate and his colleagues in the Catholic Revival had their eyes to the past, seeking the recovery of a lost medievalism with its clarity of authority and the power of a persuasive community. They sought the eloquence of poetry in its assault upon rationalism and the renewed energy of a rural simplicity. they grieved the loss of absolutes. By contrast, Lindbeck and Hauerwas have their eyes to a church of the future, anticipating tightly knit communities that will be sociologically (though not theologically) sectarian, exclusivist in their thinking and yet also ecumenical. Their quest is for a postmodern affirmation of faith on the margins, trying to articulate a new grammar of discourse, a new life of resistance, in a world where the cultured despisers of religion have long since ceased to care. Christianity today no longer needs to be defended; it has to be created anew.

This study of Allen Tate and the Catholic Revival offers an extraordinarily provocative framework for the raising of such questions. It is a splendid piece of history writing, recreating the ferment of intellectual themes that occupied the minds of the best American Catholic thinkers between the 1930s and the 1950s. With uncommon clarity, it probes the enduring question of Christianity's ongoing relationship to its culture.

It seems especially fitting to me that this book grows out of Peter Huff's work at Saint Louis University and its contribution through the years to the tradition of American Catholic thought. Philip Gleason, in his recent work on Catholic higher education, emphasizes the important role played by Saint Louis Jesuits like Joseph Husslein, Daniel Lord, Calvert Alexander, and William McGucken in the mid-century Catholic cultural revival. Peter Huff honors these who have gone before him in the best possible way, by expressing in his own careful scholarship their distinctive commitment to the "Great Tradition."

Belden C. Lane
Professor of Theological Studies and American Studies
Saint Louis University

Acknowledgments

This book is a study of a writer deeply committed to what he called the "republic of letters." In the course of writing the book I have often been reminded of my own membership in that commonwealth and my obligations to many of its leading citizens.

My teachers at Mercer University in Atlanta aroused my interest in the critical study of religious history. To Colin Harris, William Geren, Duane Davis, Carol Gates, Matthew Mancini, and Henry Curry I owe a debt of gratitude I will never be able to repay. Under their tutelage I began examining the intriguing subject of religion's various responses to the challenges of modernity. During that period I also read widely in the works of Paul Tillich. Readers familiar with his thought will see that Tillich's categories of the "broken myth" and the "vanishing of the concrete god," articulated in *Dynamics of Faith* (1957), have subtly informed my discussion of Allen Tate's theology of culture. Likewise, Timothy George, Bill J. Leonard, E. Glenn Hinson, and Leon McBeth at Southern Baptist Theological Seminary figured importantly in my education. Profoundly dedicated to the place of historical studies in the theological enterprise, they taught me something of the romance and grandeur of that discipline. At Indiana University my teachers in religious studies, American studies, and English provided exemplary models of rigorous academic integrity and imaginative interdisciplinary scholarship. J. Samuel Preus, Richard Miller, Cynthia Cinnard, Herbert Marks, Jane Rubin, and Mary Jo Weaver each made a significant impact on my work. It was my privilege to serve as Stephen J. Stein's assistant in research and classroom teaching. Whatever is of enduring worth in this study is due in large part to my association with him.

This study originated as a doctoral dissertation at Saint Louis University. Colleagues, friends, and teachers in historical theology, American studies, English, and history provided valuable assistance from the beginning of the project to its final completion. Ronald Modras, Gerard Magill, Kenneth Parker, and J. J. Mueller, S.J., stimulated my interest in modern Catholic thought. Helen Mandeville, Albert

Montesi, James Hitchcock, Thomas Knipp, and Walter J. Ong, S.J., generously enhanced my understanding of the Fugitive-Agrarians, the New Critics, and the milieu of the Catholic Revival. In numerous ways William M. Shea has been an inspiration. His instructive advice greatly enlarged my perspective on the subject of this study. I am especially grateful to my mentor, Belden C. Lane. I have profited immensely from his example as engaging writer, ecumenical churchman, interdisciplinary scholar, and faithful friend.

Many people have kindly read portions of the book. J. J. Mueller, Thomas Knipp, James Hitchcock, Ann Astell, Joseph Schwartz, Stephen Werner, and Dana Mellis read early drafts of certain sections. I thank them for their critical observations and helpful suggestions. I alone am responsible for the text in its present form. Portions of this material have appeared elsewhere. A provisional draft of the study appeared in *Humanitas* 8 (1995): 26-43. A section of chapter 3 was published in *Modern Age* 37 (Spring 1995): 226-232.

Writing such a book would have been impossible without the expert assistance of librarians and archivists at Washington University, Saint Louis University, the University of Minnesota, Princeton University, Vanderbilt University, and the University of Puget Sound. In particular, Margaret M. Sherry at Princeton and Marice Wolfe at Vanderbilt have made distinctive contributions to the book. Mrs. Helen H. Tate has been a tremendous source of support during all phases of the research. For their permission to quote from previously unpublished material, I wish to express my gratitude to Mrs. Tate and Father Ong. I also thank Kate Donahue for allowing me to read the unpublished correspondence between Tate and John Berryman. For the warm hospitality they showed to a wayfaring researcher, my appreciation goes to Mary and Maureen McCarte, Mary Jean Loomis, and the monks at St. Mary's Abbey in New Jersey. For her confidence in the value of the study and her constant efforts to improve it, I thank my editor, Kathleen Walsh of Paulist Press. For his insightful criticism of the text, I am indebted to John A. Coleman, S.J., general editor of the Isaac Hecker Studies in Religion and American Culture. For their daily gestures of Benedictine hospitality, I also wish to thank the administration and faculty of my new academic home, Saint Anselm College in New Hampshire. In an engaging study of the Rule of Saint Benedict, Esther de Waal has reminded us that the Benedictines brought Christian civilization to the Western world cruce, *libro et atro*—with cross, book and plow. In his own way, Allen Tate reckoned these tools the keys for a modern restoration of Christian culture.

More than anyone else, my wife Mary deserves recognition. As discerning editor, fellow researcher, and travel companion, she has brought her native intelligence and years of teaching experience to bear on my work. More importantly, she has intuitively appreciated my interest in Tate ever since our first conversation about the "lost generation" in the spring of 1991. Willing to interrupt vacations—and even our honeymoon—to explore the libraries, universities, neighborhoods, graveyards, churches, monasteries, and countryside associated with Allen Tate, she has graciously made the writing of this book an adventure I will never forget.

Just as the book was nearing completion, Mary and I lost our little boy, Martin. For myself, I know that I will never think of this book without thinking of him. Tate, who knew what it was for a parent to bury a child, spoke of how even the imperfect love of this world could teach us "how it is in heaven." Perhaps this book, forever linked to the memory of one of heaven's newest residents, will serve as modest testimony to our belief in the greatest republic of all, the communion of saints. Because of their unsparing devotion to the education of their son, this book is dedicated to Martin's grandparents, Walter and Jane Huff.

PAH
Saint Anselm College
Holy Week, 1996

Introduction

Poets are the mortals who...sense the trace of the fugitive gods,
stay on the gods' tracks, and so trace for their kindred mortals the
way toward the turning.

—Martin Heidegger[1]

Once a familiar figure to nearly every student of American literature
and American Catholicism, southern writer Allen Tate is now becoming something of an obscure personality in U.S. cultural history. Even
graduate students in the English departments and American studies
programs of America's major universities have trouble placing the
name or establishing its bearer's exact significance. His works have virtually disappeared from the contemporary literary canon, and his reputation has been eclipsed by a generation of critics raised on the
principles of poststructuralist experiments in literary and cultural theory. In intellectual circles where the values of deconstructionism hold
sway, Tate has not fared well. Nor has he shared the generous fate of his
contemporary William Faulkner or of his younger admirers Flannery
O'Connor and Walker Percy. Rather, he languishes in the literary limbo
reserved for writers whose concerns seem out of vogue in the age of
multiculturalism. His most famous poem, "Ode to the Confederate
Dead," written in the late 1920s, survives in anthologies and textbooks
as a landmark of literary modernism, but, offensive as it is to those who
associate the nineteenth-century Confederate States of America with
the repressive regimes of world history, it exists more as a relic than a
model. Today, Tate is primarily remembered by the professional historians of literature who preside over the southern literary establishment
and by a small circle of neo-conservative thinkers associated with periodicals of the intellectual right such as *Humanitas, Modern Age*, and *New
Oxford Review*. In the larger intellectual community, however, Tate's
unapologetic defense of high culture and the traditions of unabashed
classicism presently qualify him for exclusion from the feasts of post-
modernism. As a recent critic bluntly put it: "He was, God knows,
Eurocentric, phallocentric, logocentric, theocentric, classist, and

racist."[2] Even Tate's trademark cigarette would be banished from the sessions of the Modern Language Association.

The American academy's disregard of Tate indicates to what degree the norms of current criticism depend upon what C. S. Lewis called "chronological snobbery"—the uncritical assumption that "whatever has gone out of date is on that account discredited."[3] The backlash against Tate, while rightly questioning the literary orthodoxy established by him and his colleagues in the period between the world wars, stems in large part from American higher education's distaste for Tate's vigorous defense of the cultural value of classical Christianity. The reaction also reflects the general bias against Christianity in mainstream criticism.[4] More importantly, the negative assessment of Tate indicates a reckless misunderstanding of the important role of religion in early-twentieth-century literary criticism and the entire career of Allen Tate.

Born in the last months of the nineteenth century, the Kentucky native Allen Tate began his literary career under no such cloud. Primarily remembered today for his part in the Southern Literary Renaissance (1920–1950), the resurgence of southern letters that brought regional writers such as Faulkner and Eudora Welty to international prominence, Tate first appeared on the American literary scene as a member of Vanderbilt University's celebrated Fugitive circle, the short-lived Nashville poetry group of the 1920s that included other future greats such as John Crowe Ransom and Robert Penn Warren. After joining the postwar "lost generation" in Greenwich Village and Paris, Tate gained notoriety as a leading force within the new movement of literary modernism, the bold departure from nineteenth-century romanticism advanced by fellow expatriates Gertrude Stein, Ernest Hemingway, Ezra Pound, and T. S. Eliot. During the 1930s, while still an advocate of the *avant-garde* in literature, Tate, like many of his generation, began to register deep reservations about the values, concerns, and structures of modern culture. As a spokesman for the Southern Agrarian movement, the project of conservative social criticism that involved a number of his fellow Fugitive writers, Tate earned a reputation as a hostile though insightful interpreter of modernity, concerned most of all with what he considered the deleterious cultural consequences of industrialization and secularization. A decade later, already a formidable member of modern America's emerging literary establishment, he served as a principal architect for the movement called New Criticism, the formalist school of literary theory that revolutionized the academic study of literature and dominated the American university classroom from the 1940s to the 1960s. Though never a professional academic in the narrow sense of the term, Tate built a career largely shaped by a series of teaching assignments at universities such as Princeton, New York, Minnesota, Chicago, Oxford, and Rome. Picturing himself more properly as an independent "man of letters," he published over the course of fifty years numerous books of poems and essays, two biographies, one novel, and scores of reviews. The recipient of many awards and honors, he also distinguished himself as an editor, lecturer, translator, and statesman in the "republic of letters." By his death in 1979, though intellectual fashions had already changed dramatically, few members of the literary commonwealth failed to number him among "the major figures in modern American art."[5]

Despite the conspiracy of neglect that currently obscures his importance in American intellectual culture, one event in Tate's life remains an intriguing episode in modern literary history: his conversion to Roman Catholicism. One of a number of "lost-generation" literary converts to Catholicism, Tate entered the Catholic Church in 1950, after a twenty-year quest for a satisfying faith which led him far beyond the culturally dominant evangelical Protestantism of his geographic region. Critical of what he perceived as the dehumanizing trends of modern life, he sought in the Catholic tradition the solution to the intellectual and social problems of secular modernity. As poetic modernist, Southern Agrarian social theorist, and formalist New Critic, Tate appropriated classic Catholic themes, hoping to synthesize traditional Catholicism and aesthetic modernism into a Christian humanism revitalizing contemporary culture. At the height of his career, he functioned as the unique kind of literary figure that William Dean has called the religious critic—the public intellectual who concentrates on the place of religious tradition in culture and the meaning and health of the nation's spiritual character.[6] Representative of the "intellectual convert" that church historian John Tracy Ellis recognized as the exception to American Catholicism's dismal record of intellectual achievement,[7] Tate aspired to the role of the American Catholic critic whose work would embody the highest standards of his craft and witness to the moral authority of his adopted faith.

The famous convert Jacques Maritain believed that Tate would "serve as a guide to many among the intellectual youth of America."[8] His contemporary, the priest-critic William Lynch, reportedly thought him "one of the most Catholic minds in America," the possessor of an "extraordinary vocation" in the church.[9] Likewise, shortly after Tate's conversion, Jesuit scholar Walter Ong judged him "an exceedingly zealous and inspiringly humble Catholic" who would undoubtedly contribute to the republic of American Catholic letters.[10] Fellow convert Marshall

McLuhan, the brilliant media critic, even prophesied that Tate's would be "the nearest American equivalent to Newman's conversion."[11]

Allen Tate, however, was no Newman. As the English cardinal himself put it, "Saints are not literary men."[12] While preparing his biography of Tate during the 1960s, Radcliffe Squires wrote to the subject of his study informing him that "I don't know what to do about your relationship to the Roman Catholic Church."[13] The fact is, curiously, that neither did Tate. Naturally at home in the cosmopolitan world of literature and plagued by chronic personal problems that led him through three marriages, the convert Tate lived a life which, according to one observer, was "a poor advertisement for the Catholic faith."[14] His self-confessed "problems as a Catholic writer" prevented him from becoming the kind of religious critic he longed to be.[15] Though he endeavored to give currency to the Catholic tradition in contemporary literature, Tate was never recognized as an exemplary practitioner of his faith nor honored as a model of the ideal Catholic writer. Unlike that of John Henry Newman, the iconic convert of the previous century, Allen Tate's Catholic experience was one of gain and loss.

Tate's complex relationship to Catholicism can best be described as the consequence of a fateful affiliation with the Catholic Literary Revival, the early twentieth-century flowering of Catholic intellectual life that many thought analogous to the cultural achievements of the Christian Middle Ages. Also known as the Catholic Intellectual Renaissance, the wave of renewed interest among Western intellectuals in the Catholic religion stimulated a spirit of confidence within the Catholic community that characterized the church's experience for nearly half a century. Tate identified strongly with the movement's vision of a new Christendom and viewed his religious criticism as a contribution toward the advance of a revived Catholic humanism addressing the needs of the modern world.

The mid-century entrance of U.S. Catholicism into mainstream American culture, however, coupled with the destabilizing experience of the Second Vatican Council (1962–1965), subverted the Revival's drive for a distinctively Catholic cultural renaissance. With his spiritual fortunes tied to those of the Catholic Revival, Tate was displaced by historical forces transforming the nature of modern Catholic mission and identity. While he never experienced the kind of "deconversion" discussed in John Barbour's examination of the narratives of lost faith,[16] his Catholic experience was laced with a strange sense of alienation. What Gary Wills said of Malcolm Muggeridge in *Bare Ruined Choirs* applies equally well to Tate: "Just when he was rediscovering Christianity as a stick to beat the modern world with," the public meaning and private practice of "the most intransigent form of that faith" were undergoing a dramatic transformation unique in modern history.[17] Heidegger said that the poet in destitute times pursues the "trace of the fugitive gods."[18] In the irony and anxiety of his time, Allen Tate's Catholic quest proved even the most appealing deities fugitive.

This book argues that Tate's attraction to the values of the Catholic Revival contributed to his acceptance of the Catholic religion as well as, ironically, to his eventual sense of alienation from the church. It endeavors to assess the impact of the international Revival on Tate's religious imagination and his insecure place in the twentieth-century community of American Catholic intellectuals. Shaped by the Revival's unique history, from its rise in the anti-Catholic climate of the 1920s to its dissipation in post-World War II pluralism, Tate's troubled Catholic quest sheds light on the dilemma of the intellectual convert and the crisis of the lay apostolate in an era of shifting symbols, fleeting loyalties, and moral uncertainty.

Though hardly the product of a religious writer in the conventional sense of the term, Tate's work is of such a nature that a full comprehension of his overall critical project invites analysis of his religious discourse and aims. Consensus among his interpreters confirms that he performed his criticism "in the realm of ideas where literature, morals and politics exist side by side."[19] Writing just after the period of Tate's greatest influence upon literary criticism, R. K. Meiners claimed that "Tate's sensibility is fundamentally religious...his major developments, both as a poet and a critic, have been worked out of a religiously conceived matrix of ideas."[20] Building upon Meiners' suggestion, this study reads Tate's criticism from a fresh angle of interpretation, approaching it as a distinctive form of religious criticism, the genre of criticism that Harold Bloom defines as "a mode of description, analysis, and judgment that seeks to bring us closer to the workings of the religious imagination."[21] Interpreting his efforts as exploratory gestures toward an imaginative theology of culture, it attempts to understand Tate's critical project from the perspective of what Hans Urs von Balthasar has identified as a specific "lay style" in Christian thought stretching from Dante to Charles Péguy.[22]

In its tone, methods, and aim, my study aspires to exemplify those qualities of humanistic scholarship that southern historian C. Vann Woodward has called the "rare combination of detachment and sympathy."[23] While Tate's legacy encourages the contemporary reader to reconsider the intrinsic worth of the intellectual standards of the past and the now hotly contested notion of a hierarchy of values, it also gives a society sensitive to issues of racism, sexism, and elitism much to ponder. Likewise, my portrait of the Catholic Church and its twentieth-century trials does not attempt to enter what sociologist Gene Burns has accurately described as the already overly "politicized" discourse charging the discussion of Catholicism's recent past.[24] Rather, it is designed to stimulate curiosity about a much misunderstood period in American Catholic history and to formulate alternative ways for contemporary historiography to narrate the meaning of the entire twentieth-century Catholic experience.

This study centers on a biographical exegesis of Tate's works of prose criticism. An exercise in both intellectual biography and the burgeoning field of Catholic cultural studies, it examines the clash between tradition and modernity revealed in the experience of one figure. At the heart of Tate's experience was the confrontation with the consequences of modernity, or what the writers of the Catholic Revival almost universally described as the "crisis of the modern world." Capitalizing upon the paradoxical meaning of the term "modernism" (the experimental movement in early twentieth-century aesthetics often highly critical of the shortcomings of the modern culture to which it contributed), this study depicts Tate as a literary modernist at odds with the main currents of modernity. Placing Tate's religious criticism in the tradition of American antimodernism already established by the turn of the century,[25] I shall argue that Tate's cultural antimodernism, ironically a product of his literary modernism, was the feature of his thought that functioned as a crucial link to the values and representatives of the Catholic Revival.

The first chapter argues the necessity of interpreting the formation of Tate's religious imagination in the context of the twentieth-century Catholic Revival's peculiar history. The next two chapters analyze the significance of Tate's antimodernism and anti-industrialism in his journey toward Roman Catholicism. In those sections I make the case that Tate's countercultural intellectual commitments of the 1920s and 1930s functioned as something of a *praeparatio evangelica*. The fourth chapter, dealing with the years immediately surrounding his conversion, concentrates on Tate's efforts at performing an identifiably Catholic form of criticism. This chapter features the important place of an appropriated Neo-Thomistic perspective in Tate's version of New Criticism. The last chapter considers the contribution of a diminishing Catholic Revival mentality to Tate's apparent failure to construct a model for Catholic cultural criticism in light of the needs of modern America.

1 | A World About to Fall

After an interval of a few generations the mental climate proves unfavorable to notions of the deity which at an earlier date were perfectly satisfactory; the older gods have fallen below the common secular level, and can no longer be believed in.

—William James[1]

One of America's greatest men of letters, southern writer Allen Tate performed the function of the religious critic in an era of extraordinary social and intellectual change. In an early critical essay, first published in 1928, he explored the implications of the writer's confrontation with modernity. He identified "the perfect literary situation," the moment of prime creativity for a writer, as the unique historical condition when a previously dominant culture is about to give way to a new, more vigorous culture rising to replace it. The tension between two opposing ways of seeing the world, according to Tate, was the most fortuitous occasion for authentic art and literature. Focusing on the nineteenth century, Tate located the achievement of poet Emily Dickinson at such a fateful moment. Living in the twilight of the old Puritan theocracy, he said, Dickinson felt the portending rattle of what Oliver Wendell Holmes facetiously called the once-sturdy "deacon's masterpiece" of the culture's standing Calvinist order. Continuing well into the century, she also sensed the roar of a new industrial age gilded with transcendental optimism. No fan of Emerson's hospitable universe, Tate attributed Dickinson's convincing poetic voice not to the fact that she wrote at the dawning of a transformed New England culture, but rather to her position in "the clash of powerful opposites." Poised at the instant when "a spiritual community is breaking up," he said, the poet's prophetic instincts allow him to reveal a passing tradition's moral limitations while living off the store of its accumulated riches. "The poet finds himself," Tate explained, "balanced upon the moment when such a world is about to fall." It is precisely this precarious situation, Tate maintained, that "produces, because it is rare, a special and perhaps the most distinguished kind of poet."[2]

In his landmark study of the first southern modernists, Daniel Joseph Singal has used Tate's construct of the "perfect literary situation" to link his creative role in the Southern Literary Renaissance to the cultural shake-up that he experienced in his own regional homeland. The period of the New South into which Tate was born witnessed the rapid and pivotal shift of southern culture toward alignment with national goals and away from the post–Civil War inclination toward a distinctively sectional culture. Born out of the ashes of failed Reconstruction policies, the New South period signaled the beginning of an astonishing decay of an American regionalism that had once granted the nation an incredible degree of cultural pluralism simply by virtue of geography. Industrialization and urbanization made significant inroads into the socio-economic structure of the region, as the sentimental reconciliation of aging Federal and Confederate veterans vividly symbolized the deteriorating faith in what Charles Reagan Wilson has called the once pervasive Lost Cause civil religion.[3] Likewise, the massive migration of thousands of blacks from the rural South's agricultural backwaters to the promising manufacturing centers of the urban North, coupled with the first stirrings of the modern civil rights movement, marked a breakup of cultural and racial patterns previously imagined inexorable. One of the last great articulators of Eugene Genovese's "southern tradition" of American conservatism,[4] Tate came of age in an era of American history when society was radically altered by what some have called the second reconstruction of his region. According to Singal, Tate's attachment to a culture undergoing such profound change helps to account for the high degree of originality in his work. By the mid-1930s, he says, when Tate's career as an apologist for things southern was at its peak, Tate "had come to perceive that the South of his day was undergoing the same sort of cultural transit Emily Dickinson had experienced in New England and that it was this 'crossing of the ways' that had given rise to the 'curious burst of intelligence' so evident in southern letters."[5]

Tate's image of "the perfect literary situation" can also yield appreciable gains when applied to another dimension of his experience: the place of religion in his life and work. When Tate entered the Roman Catholic Church, a particular pattern of Catholic spirituality that seemed to grant stability in the turbulent modern age was imperceptibly in the process of decline. Long attracted to the classical Catholicism of ritual order, formal doctrine, spiritual discipline, and countercultural social witness, Tate witnessed an era of profound changes in the

Catholic Church. In fact, his conversion coincided with the radical transformation of virtually every aspect of Roman Catholic life. Just as he saw
the "One-hoss Shay" South of his racial memory breaking down even as
the engine of the New South was building steam, the Catholic tradition
he came to admire early in his career proved to be a spiritual vehicle
already rickety when he climbed aboard. The grinding dissonance of
new and old Catholicisms colliding in his experience contributes to a
fuller understanding not only of Tate's ambivalence toward religion, but
also of his inescapable fascination with it, for it sets the irony of Allen
Tate's Catholic history within its native context: the rise and fall of a
world of Catholic meaning.

"Heading Towards Catholicism"

Though he was baptized in 1950, as early as 1929 Tate began to evidence serious interest in the Catholic religion. As a Guggenheim fellow in
Europe, among the expatriate literati of the day, not yet thirty years of
age, he wrote home to a young Vanderbilt University colleague with some
shocking news. "I am more and more heading towards Catholicism," he
informed his friend Donald Davidson. "We have reached a condition of
the spirit where no further compromise is possible."[6]

That same year, writing for T. S. Eliot's new critical journal *Criterion*,
Tate articulated an argument that would become a standard theme in
his literary and social theory. Convinced that modern society had
reached an alarming state of cultural degeneration, he maintained that
"an objective religion, a universal scheme of reference," was necessary
for the survival of Western civilization. Though he insisted that his position entailed "in no sense a confession of faith" privileging a specific
religious tradition, his next few publications clearly demonstrated that
the anonymous "universal scheme of reference" shared much in common with the faith of Roman Catholicism.[7]

Feeling an attraction to the Catholic Church in the Roman Jubilee
year 1929 meant appreciating a religious tradition unapologetically
dogmatic and avowedly illiberal. The Lateran Treaty of that year, for
instance, rejected the notion of the exclusively spiritual nature of papal
authority and reaffirmed the pope's claim to temporal power over the
Vatican territory. Only recently free from association with Action
Française, the monarchist movement led by French traditionalist cru-
sader Charles Maurras, the church on the eve of the Great Depression
also found itself newly entangled with Opus Dei, the controversial
movement of Spanish origin promoting aggressive lay involvement in

right-wing political ventures. It was a church which proscribed involvement in the fledgling ecumenical movement, obliged its clergy to forswear modernist thoughts, denounced the liberal "hypothesis" of church-state separation, prohibited the use of artificial birth-control methods among its laity, legislated precise norms of proper dress for female communicants, and censored new motion pictures along with an already long Index of Forbidden Books.

In the United States, rudely reminded of its tenuous status by presidential candidate Alfred E. Smith's political defeat, the church remained discredited in intellectual quarters by Pius IX's earlier *Syllabus of Errors* and Leo XIII's 1899 condemnation of "Americanism," controversial papal pronouncements that seemed to reinforce Rome's age-old reputation for authoritarianism and obscurantism. The perception of American Catholic opposition to the republican Popular Front battling General Franco's fascist forces in the Spanish Civil War a few years later only served to validate that conclusion for non-Catholic American progressives. Drawing from a venerable tradition of anti-Catholic polemic reaching back to the eschatological musings of seventeenth-century Puritan divines, critics now ranked "Romanism" in the same category as the fundamentalist rabble that put Dayton, Tennessee on the cultural map. In the heyday of American progressivism, no better example of hidebound resistance to modern civilization could be found than the Roman Catholic Church.

More than the sum of its detractors' aspersions, however, the church that originally appealed to Tate represented for many adherents a vibrant atmosphere of meaning in stark contrast to the spiritual aridity of modern culture and the thin air of liberal Protestantism. For ordinary American Catholics raised in rural and urban working-class communities, a "devotional Catholicism,"[8] forged during the nineteenth-century immigrant experience, functioned as a complex system of ritual observances that granted unambiguous identity by setting them apart from their non-Catholic neighbors. Paired with the supernatural world view of classical Christianity, it immersed them in what was advertised as an unbroken chain of tradition connecting their experience with that of the original Christian apostles. Latin masses, meatless Fridays, Marian parades, parish missions, parochial schools, auricular confession, catechetical instruction, and countless acts of piety in public and domestic settings defined the boundaries of the largely self-contained Catholic community's sacred cosmos.[9] According to sociologists Roger Finke and Rodney Stark, the official church of the period offered Catholic Americans "an intense faith with a vivid sense of otherworldliness." It "created an encapsulated social structure—a kind of parallel Catholic America."[10]

For educated Catholics of the time, the church held certain attractions for the life of the mind. The official church philosophy of Neo-Thomism, retrieving for modern readers the rigorous system of the thirteenth-century "angelic doctor" Thomas Aquinas, provided resilient defense against the perceived anti-intellectualism of popular culture and the much discussed positivism of the secular academy. Describing itself as the true heir to the Western intellectual tradition, the neo-scholastic "synthesis" reigned in the seminaries and imbued a rising middle class of literate Catholic lay people with a sense of intellectual certainty in the intimidating context of modern society's competitive marketplace of ideas. Likewise, recent papal encyclicals addressing current economic issues of labor and capital fueled Catholic enthusiasm for an aggressive "reconstruction of the social order." Contributing to the formation of a genuinely Catholic Social Gospel, social theorists on both sides of the Atlantic attempted to introduce academic and political audiences to the relevance of a "public Catholicism" shaped by papal moral teaching.[11] Motivated by the new conception of a lay apostolate, envisioning the laity as the activist arm of the modern church, Catholic members of the work force took their faith into their "temporal" vocations. At the same time, a new generation of aspiring Catholic professionals pursued their tasks with firm dedication yearning for the conception of a new Christian culture approximating or even surpassing the achievements of medieval Christendom. It was the high point of a period in modern Catholic experience known as the Catholic Revival. For a sympathetic observer like Tate, the church of the Revival era seemed to promise access to the accumulated wisdom and beauty of the Western heritage within a spiritually stimulating environment, precisely at the moment when that heritage was severely threatened by rival views of the proper place of religion in culture.

The Catholic Revival   *1890-1960*

The Catholic Revival was a distinctive chapter in modern Catholic intellectual history stretching roughly from the death of Newman in 1890 to the years immediately preceding John XXIII's announcement of the Second Vatican Council in 1959. It marked an extraordinary "Catholic moment" in the first decades of the twentieth century, particularly those between the world wars, when a resurgence of Catholic literary activity took on the appearance of a surprising season of *kairos* in

Catholic experience. To those sympathetic with its motives and goals, it promised a revitalization of Catholic intellectual life extensive enough to reverse the effects of modern secularization and return the Western world to a religiously homogeneous culture permeated throughout with Christian values.[12]

Primarily, the Revival was an international movement comprising a variety of trends and individual efforts in Europe and North America, all of which emphasized the diverse cultural resources of the historic Catholic heritage and the contemporary social relevance of traditional Catholic thought. Led by a small minority of intellectual elites—lay, religious, and clerical—the movement sought to foster "a new synthesis of Christian faith and life, a Christian humanism, rooted in and continuous with the tradition of the church, but responsive to the modern world."[13] According to *Commonweal*, the lay-run American Catholic weekly, the Revival encompassed a wide spectrum of Catholic life:

> the revival of Scholastic philosophy, the increase of higher education generally among Catholics, the enrichment and strengthening of art and letters and science, the bringing to bear of Catholic principles and even of Catholic methods upon modern economic problems...the tremendous growth of missionary activities, [and] the outpouring of new manifestations of mysticism and spiritual devotions, particularly among the laity.[14]

Concerned above all with the issue of historical continuity, many participants in the Catholic Revival sought to locate their labors in a larger context by tracing the roots of their movement to the widespread renewal of interest in classical Christianity that accompanied the romantic movement in Europe after the French Revolution. The rediscovery of Catholic sacrament and dogma and the positive reevaluation of the legacy of the Middle Ages, characteristic of nineteenth-century developments such as the Oxford Movement in England, were especially significant to advocates of the twentieth-century Revival. In fact, the first historians to make definitive use of the term "Catholic Revival" were Catholic writers at the turn of the century anxious to establish continuity with the nineteenth-century "heroic age" of Catholicism.[15]

The European Catholic Intellectual Renaissance

The main impetus for the Catholic Revival was a literary resurgence among European Catholic writers in the early 1900s. An impressive number of poets, novelists, dramatists, artists, journalists, historians, and philosophers proudly identified themselves as Catholic during those years. Moreover, they insisted that Roman Catholicism was responsible for everything glorious in the Western world's history and all that proved promising in its future. As one propagandist for the Revival put it: "The Faith is Europe, and Europe is the Faith."[16] In France, the achievements of George Bernanos, Léon Bloy, Paul Claudel, François Mauriac, Charles Péguy, Emmanuel Mounier, Julian Green, Etienne Gilson, and Jacques and Raissa Maritain signaled the commencement of a new age for Catholic letters and the rescue of a national church threatened with virtual irrelevance. Similarly, G. K. Chesterton, Hilaire Belloc, Christopher Dawson, Eric Gill, Graham Greene, Ronald Knox, E. I. Watkin, Christopher Hollis, Martin D'Arcy, and Evelyn Waugh helped to revitalize England's literary life and its struggling Catholic culture.

With the exception of a few professional academicians, most of the Revival writers functioned as old-fashioned "men of humane letters," intellectual humanists directly engaged in society's artistic and public life rather than cloistered, technical research. A study of Chesterton's work, for example, rightly calls him a "philosopher without portfolio."[17] Even the university-trained and -employed scholars among them, such as Dawson and Maritain, entertained liberal interpretations of the scholarly vocation, enjoying a wide readership outside academic circles. Extremely prolific, most of the writers displayed incredible versatility, demonstrating command of issues across a formidable spectrum of subject matter, ranging from social criticism and economic theory to ethics and aesthetics. Many of the most popular wrote in multiple genres, publishing in a single career volumes of non-fiction, verse, and fiction, light and serious. A few lesser lights of the Revival, too eagerly applying Catholic apologetics to fields outside their competence, were dismissed as mere dilettantes.

Speaking specifically of the writers of the English Revival, Adrian Hastings has captured the tenor of the Revival literature. Most of the main figures in the movement, he says,

> steered clear of theology in any very exact sense and very few...had the slightest worry about ultramontanism. In a critical sense they were rather ahistorical and atheological: that is to say they accepted the current Roman Catholic position in doctrine and practice as almost unquestionably right in all its details, and argued accordingly. Its very authoritativeness was what appealed. They found in it a sure framework for spiritual progress, literary creativity and political stability, but also for an ordered and

coherent view of the world to replace the increasing intellectual and ideological confusion outside the walls.[18]

Characterized by an independent and urbane style of conservatism espousing deep affection for the tradition of Catholicism yet often aloof toward ecclesiastical politics, the Catholic Revival produced a paradoxical strain of spirituality unique in twentieth-century Catholicism: traditionalist and polemical on the one hand, worldly and tolerant on the other.

The Role of Converts in the Revival

An important dimension of the Catholic Literary Revival was the role played by distinguished converts in the Revival's leadership. Just as the renewal of Catholicism in the nineteenth century depended in large part on the gifts of its educated adult converts, the twentieth-century Catholic Revival may best be remembered for the astounding spate of intellectual and literary conversions it generated. In fact, some of the most prominent writers of the European Revival—Claudel, the Maritains, Chesterton, Greene, Knox, Waugh, and Dawson—were converts to the Catholic faith. Even the reputation of sympathetic non-Catholics, such as "near-converts" Henri Bergson, Alfred North Whitehead, and Simone Weil, along with that of Anglican converts W. H. Auden, T. S. Eliot, and C. S. Lewis, added lustre to the achievements of the Revival.[19] As Hilaire Belloc put it, "the more powerful, the more acute, and the more sensitive minds of our time are clearly inclining toward the Catholic side."[20] For the first time since the Counter-Reformation, as another observer noted, conversions were flowing not away from Catholicism but toward it.[21]

Though the converts of the Revival sought the Catholic faith for a variety of reasons, their individual experiences usually revolved around a cluster of classic concerns at odds with the trends of modernity: the search for beauty in a world of industrial ugliness, the desire for mystery in a world of cold rationalism, the pursuit of truth in a world of relativism, and a hunger for infallible authority in a world of sure uncertainty. Ronald Knox summed up the various motives for conversion as so many expressions of a modern quest for tradition:

> More and more, I think, as the changing conditions of modern society cut us off from the memory of old things; as customs die out, and property changes hands, and our language loses its virility, and even (perhaps) the power of the Empire we live in sinks

in the scale of political values, men will look towards the Catholic Church, if only as the repository of long traditions, the undying, unmoved spectator of the thousand phases and fashions that have passed over our restless world. I may be wrong, but it seems to me that it is already happening; that the reaction from all this silly worship of the future is predisposing men's minds towards the Catholic claim.[22]

While most were genuine spiritual pilgrims, some of the Revival's converts sought the church for more eccentric reasons. In one of Chesterton's popular detective stories, for example, the priest-sleuth Father Brown comments sardonically on the number of "scatter-brained sceptics" drifting to the Catholic faith in his time.[23] Likewise, the poet-protagonist of *The Man Who Was Thursday*, Chesterton's 1908 "philosophical romance," admits that conversion was something of an artistic fad: "Oh, we are all Catholics now."[24] By 1935, when the American Jesuit Calvert Alexander wrote *The Catholic Literary Revival*, he confidently recorded the fulfillment of Anglican Dean Inge's reluctant prophecy that accepting the faith of "Romanism" had become "the fashion for popular men of letters." In fact, Alexander wondered if there might be some danger that the new intellectual converts were making aesthetics "the chief reason for becoming Catholic."[25]

The Catholic Church in the United States also enjoyed its share of convert writers. Catholicism, of course, had always appealed to a few isolated individuals in the history of America's literary community.[26] In fact, the American church traditionally relied upon its educated converts to serve as apologists for the faith. In addition to the well-known converts Orestes Brownson and Isaac Hecker, editor James A. McMaster, novelist Francis Marion Crawford, Western writer Frank H. Spearman, poet Joyce Kilmer, social reformer Rose Hawthorne Lathrop, and southern humorist Joel Chandler Harris represented the small but significant group of writers who found the church of Rome an intriguing alternative to the Protestant denominations of Victorian America. In his famous essay, "American Catholics and the Intellectual Life," John Tracy Ellis credited this "small band of intellectual converts" with the few high points in nineteenth-century Catholicism's engagement with American intellectual culture.[27]

In the early twentieth century, the American church witnessed such a steady stream of notable literary conversions that the statistics tended to support Calvert Alexander's hypothesis of something suggesting a cultural trend. In 1928, citing "a very remarkable body of converts to Catholicism among college professors, social workers, writers, and scientists," *Commonweal*'s editor Michael Williams declared that "the modern mind is turning again to Catholicism."[28] Three years later, his magazine boasted an incremental increase in the number of American converts possessing "very interesting intellectual quality."[29] For Alexander, the conclusion was clear: the Catholic Church was attracting the best and brightest of the age.[30]

Born between 1890 and the close of the First World War, two genera- tions of American writers felt deeply the attraction of the Catholic faith. They found their spiritual home in the church, believing entrance into the Catholic community to be an integral part of their literary careers. Including Katherine Anne Porter, Ernest Hemingway, Dorothy Day, Thomas Merton, Robert Lax, Clare Boothe Luce, Robert Lowell, Tennessee Williams, Wallace Stevens, and Walker Percy, the American literary converts were drawn to Catholicism for intellectual and aesthet- ic reasons, motives mixing undefined spiritual aspirations with roman- tic countercultural protests.

Some, like theater critic Richard Gilman, were received into commu- nion with the church after a period of infatuation, but remained "semi- secret" Catholics, never experiencing full integration into the Catholic community.[31] Others, including literary critic Van Wyck Brooks and journalist Walter Lippmann, exhibited a "curiously Protestant flirtation with Roman Catholicism," without ever entering the church formally.[32] They were what philosopher George Santayana disparagingly called connoisseurs of Christianity.[33] According to Merton, there were many in this category:

> They stand in the stacks of libraries and turn over the pages of St. Thomas's *Summa* with a kind of curious reverence. They talk in their seminars about "Thomas" and "Scotus" and "Augustine" and "Bonaventure" and they are familiar with Maritain and Gilson, and they have read all the poems of Hopkins—and indeed they know more about what is best in the Catholic literary and philo- sophical tradition than most Catholics ever do on this earth. They sometimes go to Mass, and wonder at the dignity and restraint of the old liturgy....But they never come into the Church.[34]

By and large, the American converts knew little of the parochial life of the U.S. Catholic ethnic subculture. Like Newman before his conver- sion, they were ignorant of "the hidden life" of practicing Catholics.[35] Having minimal contact with Catholic institutions prior to their conver- sions, they made their way into Catholicism without the aid of special organizations geared to promoting conversions. The Paulist Fathers, the

Knights of Columbus, the Convert Makers of America, and the "Convert's Hour" radio program had a negligible influence on their decisions. Though they knew some fugitives from Catholicism like F. Scott Fitzgerald and Mary McCarthy, as well as some younger Catholic writers like Flannery O'Connor, the vast majority of the literary converts had few ties to Catholic authors born and raised in the faith. Rarely were they on intimate terms with members of the Catholic literary establishment such as Kathleen Norris, Lucille Papen Borden, and J. F. Powers. Generally, the Catholicism that they affirmed was a private, sometimes idiosyncratic, appropriation of what they took to be a universal system of belief and beauty, often more European than American.

Many of the converts, enticed by the exotic features of Catholic doctrine or the high drama of Roman liturgy and devotion, shared the imaginative "nostalgia for Catholic order" that Harold Bloom has found in Hemingway's literary consciousness.[36] Earlier in the century, William James had been attuned to this very "aesthetic motive." Writing in *The Varieties of Religious Experience*, he admitted that the demand of the aesthetic imagination

> makes it rigorously impossible...that Protestantism, however superior in spiritual profundity it may be to Catholicism, should at the present day succeed in making many converts from the more venerable ecclesiasticism. The latter offers a so much richer pasturage and shade for the fancy, has so many cells with so many different kinds of honey, is so indulgent in its multiform appeals to human nature, that Protestantism will always show to Catholic eyes the almshouse physiognomy.[37]

For all of the converts of the Catholic Revival, the church represented the realm of mystery sadly absent from modern experience. More than just a religion, Catholicism was for them, as Anne Roche Muggeridge has described it, "a country of the heart and of the mind."[38] Disgusted by the banal dimensions of what Merton called a "society of salesmen,"[39] they found an oasis of beauty in the divine drama of the church's worship. Critical of the reductionism of modern thought and the shallowness of liberal Protestantism, they found the integrity of Neo-Thomism and classical Christian orthodoxy intellectually stimulating. Witnessing the contemporary menace of totalitarian politics, they sought the remedy to secular society's ills in the sacred tradition of the church. Even the preconciliar church's requirement of personal sacrifice appeared as an attractive component of Catholic life. Though the converts were often drawn to the faith precisely because of orthodox Catholicism's antimodernist stance, they nevertheless expressed impatience with the Catholic ghetto's naive rejection of modern art and literature. What the American literary converts advocated was aggressive interaction with the modern world, not retreat into separatist folkways. They sought a religious tradition that would directly address the authoritative wisdom of the past to the fragmented world of the present.

As a rule, the American literary converts, like their European counterparts, followed an intellectual path into the faith. Ever since Augustine heard the child in the garden singing, "*Tolle lege, tolle lege*," people had been reading their way into the Catholic Church. But Thomas Merton's conversion, triggered by a chance encounter with Gilson's *The Spirit of Mediaeval Philosophy* in a Fifth Avenue bookstore, became nearly paradigmatic of the intellectual American's conversion before and after his time.[40] Others, born into the church, experienced an analogous rebirth of faith and religious identity after immersing themselves in the literature of the Revival. Due in large part to the transatlantic publishing enterprises of the British couple Frank Sheed and Maisie Ward, especially the 1933 opening of their New York office, educated American Catholics formed a ready audience for a flood of European Catholic literature fusing formidable literary standards with philosophical commentary steeped in traditional Catholic values. Church leaders pressed for a strong American showing in the Revival, and as early as 1929 the popular churchman Fulton J. Sheen was urging U.S. Catholic colleges and universities to "educate for a Catholic Renaissance."[41]

The Catholic Revival in America

Seriously under-represented in histories of twentieth-century Catholic intellectual and literary life, the Catholic Revival in the United States is only beginning to receive critical scrutiny as a distinct movement of intellectual activity and spirituality. It suffers from a lingering scholarly bias against the entire preconciliar period of twentieth-century Catholic history, which links it to the last stage of Tridentine Catholicism when a "complacent anti-intellectualism, reflexive anti-communism, and a repressive sexual ethic" allegedly held sway in the church.[42] Revisionist historians, too, have simply accepted the long-standing academic contempt for the period, thereby relegating the American Revival to the edges of an already marginal history.[43] Consequently, the critical study of the Revival as an American cultural phenomenon is only in its infancy. Though one may question to what extent it is legitimate to speak of a Catholic "Revival" in the United

States (skeptics would say with some justification that there was nothing to revive), historian Arnold Sparr's research has shown that there did exist a small but influential network of lay and clerical Catholics in America who hoped to augment Catholic culture by stimulating a literary flowering among their coreligionists. Motivated by the threefold desire "to promote the intellectual standing of American Catholicism, to defend the Catholic faith and its adherents from detractors, and to redeem what was seen as a drifting and fragmented secular culture," the American advocates of the Revival envisioned the fruit of their work as nothing less than the emergence of a regenerated American civilization.[44] Triggering an explosion of activity—from the founding of Catholic periodicals to the organization of Catholic learned associations and social movements—the Catholic Revival fired the imagination of a generation of American Catholics.

Sparr divides the American dimension of the Revival into three stages, charting its history over four decades of American Catholic history. The first phase, 1920–1935, involved church leaders from mainly midwestern states who sought to champion the cause of Catholic literature in the United States and deliver an intelligent apology for Catholicism in a hostile cultural climate. Like nineteenth-century intellectuals who had tried to conceive a genuinely American literary tradition, they established organizations such as the Catholic Book Club and the Catholic Poetry Society to promote quality Catholic writing and recognize worthy Catholics committed to the "apostolate of the pen." Two key leaders, Jesuits Francis X. Talbot, editor of *America* magazine, and Daniel A. Lord of Saint Louis University, initiated the American drive for the Revival from "a curious mixture of insecurity, protest, and apostolic mission."[45] Determined to show that devout Catholic faith was no barrier to rigorous intellectual achievement, they laced their concern for higher aesthetic standards among their fellow Catholics with a pattern of theological apologetics designed to show the rational and spiritual superiority of the Catholic religion. Taking another approach, *Commonweal*'s lay editors Michael Williams and George Shuster sought to avoid the crass boosterism of Lord, which appeared to judge indiscriminately all Catholic literature as necessarily excellent. While sympathetic to the dream of an American Revival, they offered realistic estimates of the efforts required to lift American Catholic intellectual capabilities to the level of international standards.[46]

The second stage of the Revival's American career witnessed the growing sophistication of a generation of U.S. Catholics coming to maturity between 1935 and 1955. The new Catholic Renascence Society, founded in 1939 with the conviction that "Catholicism is not only a creed but also a culture,"[47] continued the Revival's anxious vigilance "for the coming of a Catholic masterpiece," but it represented a level of intellectual awareness far beyond that evident in the organizations founded in the first years of the Revival. The journalist Garry Wills, himself a member of that generation, described the "fussy concern with taste" that led educated Catholics of the time to strive for even higher standards in Catholic art, literature, and liturgy. His bittersweet *Bare Ruined Choirs* (1972) communicates the almost chauvinistic pride that young Catholics displayed in their enthusiasm for Gregorian chant, papal encyclicals, and the other trappings of a fashionable "higher Catholicism."[48]

Aesthetics, however, was not the only concern of this phase of the Revival. During this period, American Catholics ardently supported various causes aimed at the reinvigoration of the U.S. church, employing as their watchwords interrelated themes from twentieth-century papal teaching: frequent communion, the apostolate of the laity, Catholic Action, and the Mystical Body of Christ. National and international conferences concerning topics such as liturgical revival, eucharistic devotion, and social justice drew large audiences of concerned Christians, contributing to the development of a new breed of activist Catholic. Lay people assumed an especially prominent role in such endeavors. A variety of lay congresses, associations, and guilds made a lay revival an enduring legacy of the Catholic Revival era.[49] Numerous "pious unions," or voluntary societies, trained lay people for the performance of the "spiritual and corporal works of mercy," as special interest groups geared toward propagation of the faith, notably the Catholic Evidence Guild organized in New York in 1931, enlisted lay persons in activities ranging from adult education to street-corner preaching. A spokesman for one such group boasted: "When the history of the twentieth century will be written it will reveal a galaxy of eminent lay leaders in the Church."[50]

The multifaceted movement of Catholic Action, defined by Pius XI as "the participation of the laity in the apostolate of the Church's hierarchy," overlapped with the impulse toward a rebirth of Catholic literary and intellectual life. Stamped with "an uncompromising laicism,"[51] Catholic Action engaged committed Catholics in enterprises designed to apply the gospel to a host of issues intricately connected to the dream of a re-Christianized culture: poverty, labor, youth, education, marriage, family, politics, and the arts. Women, conspicuously involved in all aspects of Catholic Action, contributed various resources to the cause. Modern Catholic social activism achieved its mature form in the work of leaders Dorothy Day and Baroness Catherine de Hueck. In addition, the Grail movement, tied to a retreat center for lay women located in rural Ohio, emphasized a uniquely feminine version of Revival spirituality energized by a "monastic" vision of the convergence of prayer, liturgy, labor, and artistic creativity.[52]

At the center of the ebullience were key institutions of Catholic higher learning thriving in an expansive period of American Catholic education. Attempting to instill in their students fervor for the Revival through curricular innovations, Catholic schools began offering specialized courses in the literature of the contemporary Catholic Revival. The model for such courses was that designed and taught by University of Notre Dame's Francis O'Malley. Called the Knute Rockne of the school's academic faculty by *Newsweek* magazine, the layman O'Malley taught literature on the South Bend campus from 1933 until his death in 1974. Famous for his Philosophy of Literature course for English majors, in the 1930s he introduced an elective course on Modern Catholic Writers open to university students in any field. Reflecting what would later be dubbed an interdisciplinary approach, the 200-level course's reading list included works by the established authors of the Revival: Newman, Belloc, Chesterton, Dawson, Greene, Waugh, Bernanos, Mauriac, Watkin, Gilson, and Maritain, as well as the Jesuit poet Gerard Manley Hopkins, Norwegian novelist Sigrid Undset, and continental priest-scholars Karl Adam and Romano Guardini among others.[53] At the same time, Virgil Michel, the Benedictine priest best known for his leadership in the liturgical renewal movement, also attempted to infuse American Catholic education with an appreciation for the Catholic Revival. As dean of the College of Arts and Sciences at St. John's University in Collegeville, Minnesota, Michel initiated a novel two-year program for upper-division students which endeavored "to convey a mastery of the best Christian thought" of the "Catholic Revival of Our Day."[54] Deeply dedicated to plans for educational reform, O'Malley, Michel, and other like-minded Catholic educators designed new courses to foster the wide-reaching Christian humanism typical of the Revival mentality.

The third and final phase of the American Revival entailed the gradual dissolution of the movement in the 1950s. Like all movements of religious revitalization, the Catholic Revival had its own morphology. Subject to the dynamics of growth and decline, it carried unpredictable consequences for its participants. Several factors contributed to its demise. First, many American Catholics came to see the Revival's insistence upon encouraging a Catholic cultural renaissance as simply an elaborate scheme for perpetuating remnants of the U.S. Catholic immigrant experience. Newly awakened to the beneficial possibilities of cultural pluralism, Catholics in postwar America viewed the vision of a specifically Catholic culture as narrow, provincial, and unnecessary. Second, a mood of national consensus, privileging impulses toward cultural assimilation and ecumenical harmony, cast the twin Revival themes of Catholic superiority and vulnerability in an unfavorable and peculiarly un-American light. The apologetic tone of Revival literature and the almost polemical Catholic "sense of apartness" appeared increasingly defensive, all too reminiscent of the "fortress mentality" of a minority church accused of harboring foreign loyalties and subversive sensibilities.[55]

Third, the general failure of the American Revival to produce many original thinkers of high intellectual caliber proved a great disappointment to the promoters of the movement. It exposed the weaknesses in the central strategy of the Revival itself. At best, the literature published by American Catholic writers of the time was largely derivative, amounting mainly to imitations and popularizations of superior developments in European thought. At worst, the Revival only perpetuated the reputation of American Catholicism for turning out second-rate literature. According to Paul R. Messbarger, the mediocre tradition of Catholic literature during the years of the American immigrant church "virtually precluded the growth of indigenous literary creativity" in the first half of the twentieth century.[56]

Finally, the American Revival, dependent as it was upon European developments, suffered from the waning influence of Revival forces on the other side of the Atlantic. Despite the uncontestable success of the continental Revival at producing world-class intellectuals and literature of enviable quality, the international Catholic Revival as a specific form of Christian spirituality became a casualty of the general transformation of Roman Catholic life and thought around the middle of the twentieth century.

The Transformation of Twentieth-Century Catholicism

The intellectually and aesthetically appealing form of Catholicism that Allen Tate first encountered in the Paris of the American literary expatriates survived long enough to witness his mid-century conversion. Novelist Caroline Gordon, his first wife, entered the church in 1947, and Tate followed three years later, barely a month after Pius XII's *Munificentissimus deus*, defining the dogma of the Virgin Mary's Assumption, underscored the traditional barriers separating Roman Catholicism from both the Protestant churches and modernity.

Appropriately Jacques Maritain, the premier French Neo-Thomist and for many the figure best exemplifying the vision of the Catholic Revival, served as Tate's godfather.

By the Holy Year of 1950, however, the Catholic Church was already engaged in a period of transition that would culminate in a revolutionized Catholicism inhospitable to the concerns of the Revival and nearly unrecognizable to Tate or Maritain or Pope Pius. Described by historian Jay P. Dolan as the beginning of the modern "Catholic Reformation" that gave rise to a "new Catholicism,"[57] an era of change and controversy brought to an end not only a discrete chapter of modern Catholic history, but also the Catholic Revival's short-lived attempt to extend Catholic thought into the high culture of modern Western society. Usually associated with the upheaval surrounding the Second Vatican Council (1962–1965), what many have designated as "the decisive ecclesial event of the twentieth century,"[58] the transformation of twentieth-century Catholicism originated before the convention of the Council and eventually surpassed the moderate reforms approved by the official Council fathers. Growing out of the postwar discontent with standardized forms of devotion, the varieties of postconciliar spirituality emphasized a set of assumptions concerning the purpose of the church and the relation of religion to culture at variance with views that had governed Catholic reflection on such subjects only decades before. Theologically, the situation was not much different. As Avery Dulles has observed, the Council "contributed to a new theological climate in which novelty was not only tolerated but glorified."[59] Revisionist thinkers gained prominence in the church's theological community and radically redefined the agenda for professional theology in the second half of the twentieth century. Progressives hailed the new era as a triumph of theological pluralism, while conservative critics feared the consequences of unrestrained moral, intellectual, liturgical, and disciplinary permissiveness. Aside from the strictly institutional changes that Vatican II represented and the theological re-evaluations that it stimulated, the Council can perhaps best be described as a convenient event by which to date "the dissolution of a distinct Catholic culture."[60]

What disappeared in the wake of the Vatican Council was more than a "preconciliar" church definable only in pejorative terms—a "Pius epoch," as Karl Rahner called it, of negative uniformity.[61] Rather, despite its conspicuous limitations, it was a highly imaginative world of myth, meaning, and ritual, based upon the classical vision of Catholicism's cultural mission. As Timothy McCarthy has stated, "The preconciliar church offered Catholics a religion of beauty, order, and goodness, however imperfectly realized."[62] Concerned in its essence with the spiritual and cultural re-creation of Western civilization, the Catholic Revival was a religious revitalization movement courageously attempting the ever elusive goal of conjoining contemplation and action. Not everything constitutive of the pre-Vatican II church was part of the Catholic Revival, of course, nor did everything in the postconciliar church serve to diminish such an heroic sense of Catholic culture. But the church between the two Vatican Councils functioned as the host environment for a remarkable and brief flourishing of the life of the Catholic mind. A world about to fall, it was the Catholicism that once seemed to the young Allen Tate the "universal scheme of reference."

2 | The Oldest Fundamentalism in the World

You get hold of a beautiful intuition and immediately antagonize your followers by founding a Church thereon; when the probability is, you have stopped considerably short of the core of truth and are naming some accidental relation or other as THE FUNDAMENTALS.
                                        —John Crowe Ransom to Allen Tate[1]

According to a popular interpretation of twentieth-century Catholic history, the Second Vatican Council represented the Roman Catholic Church's official, though belated, reconciliation with modernity. The church read the "signs of the times," so the interpretation goes, and found modernity a rather hospitable environment for the Christian gospel. Despite the oversimplified perspective of such a view, it does accurately take into account the church's notable abandonment of a mode of theological rhetoric that aggressively pitted Christianity against modernity. Clearly, the tone and substance of the conciliar documents demonstrated the degree to which the Catholic polemic against the modern world, routinely criticized by prominent Protestant theologians, was moved to the periphery of official Catholic discourse. Perhaps no other phenomenon so dramatically measures the degree of intellectual transformation in the twentieth-century Catholic mind than the church's loss of its once characteristic antimodern animus.

When Allen Tate first encountered the Catholic Revival, a salient feature of the movement was its negative assessment of modern culture. Advocating a creative encounter between Catholicism and the secular world, the Revival nevertheless opposed many of the social and philosophical currents of modernity. In fact, it was a commonplace of the Catholic Revival that the world produced by the sixteenth century had unleashed destructive tendencies in modern life and chaotic trends in modern thought. Informed by a distinctive philosophy of historical decline, negating the popular Enlightenment notion of inevitable progress, the Catholic Revival produced a rather bleak portrait of the

25

modern world. To the writers of the Revival, modernity was the result of vast cultural disintegration, the massive fragmentation and distortion of vital institutions stretching back to Christian and classical antiquity. Sharing an international mood of cultural pessimism most forcefully articulated in *The Decline of the West* (1918, 1922), the massive two-volume classic of antimodernism by German intellectual Oswald Spengler,[2] they contributed to the elaboration of an apocalyptic vision of history, mitigated only by the hope that Christianity would soon regain its cultural hegemony. Though they disagreed over the appropriate strategy for engineering such a cultural revitalization, the Revival writers demonstrated remarkable consistency in their analysis of the origins and consequences of modernity. The product of the intellectual and social ferment marking the Renaissance-Reformation era, modernity shattered the Christian "synthesis" of medieval culture, thereby threatening both the survival of meaningful community and the future of authentic Christianity. The Revival pictured the modern age as spiritually destitute and, therefore, intrinsically hostile to the well-being of human culture and true religion.

By virtue of this strain in its thought, the Catholic Revival was part of a larger movement of antimodernist criticism, or countermodernism, rising during the late nineteenth century and cresting during the middle decades of the twentieth. In the United States, it profited from a tradition of antimodern social analysis dating back to figures such as Orestes Brownson and Henry Adams. Along with their European counterparts and other, non-Catholic, critics of modern society, the intellectuals of the U.S. Catholic Revival objected to the uncompromising turbulence of the modern experience that made "nervousness" the privileged affliction in *fin-de-siècle* America and insecurity the premier emotional state of W. H. Auden's twentieth-century "Age of Anxiety."[3]

American Jesuit Bakewell Morrison, for instance, railed against the frantic temper of modern living, especially the unhealthy pace that kept modern urbanites "perpetually rushing about in search of they know not what."[4] With sentiments anticipating the classic mid-century critiques of technological high modernism, such as David Riesman's *The Lonely Crowd* (1950), William Whyte's *The Organizational Man* (1956), and Herbert Marcuse's *One-Dimensional Man* (1964), Morrison and his colleagues lamented the late industrial age's excessive individualism, its hollow consumerism, and its tragic loss of public life. They especially protested what they perceived to be the depersonalization of human life caused by modernization. Drawing from a growing treasury of conventional complaints, the Revival critics faulted modernity with simultaneously unsettling and over-regulating the affairs of everyday life. Modernity, they asserted, transformed ordinary life into a mechanized existence—impoverished by the commercialization of society and imprisoned by what Max Weber described as the "iron cage" of the modern economic order. The noise of modern industry suggested the death rattle of a once vibrant society, while the landscape of the urban West brought to their imaginations the rubble of a vanquished civilization. Interpreted according to theological categories, the rise of the intrusive, bureaucratic state and the triumph of standardized, mass culture in the marketplace seemed to be the apocalyptic epiphanies of a new barbaric idolatry.

The antagonism toward modernity was registered most clearly in the Catholic Revival's antipathy toward modern thought. Catholic writers on both sides of the Atlantic routinely targeted rationalism, naturalism, secularism, subjectivism, scientism, positivism, and other contemporary "isms" as the mental diseases plaguing and polluting the minds of moderns. As one of Chesterton's characters frankly put it, "The most dangerous criminal now is the entirely lawless modern philosopher."[5] Advancing the thesis that the career of Protestantism in Western history had actually promoted the advent of unbelief in modern society, popular religion textbooks for undergraduates in Catholic colleges, such as those written by Morrison, made the case that the Western mind was in a state of horrible confusion. Given the disorientation of the modern mind, particularly its paradoxical propensity to distrust reason while simultaneously overvaluing it, these texts warned contemporary students of the intellectual "vagueness and unbelief" that lurked "without the portals of the Catholic Church."[6] Recognizing the extremes within modern thought, other writers earmarked Catholicism as the corrective to the inordinate claims of both sides of secular intellectual culture: the "Age of Reason" and the modern "Revolt Against Reason."[7]

The Catholic Revival found official endorsement of its antimodernism in the church's authoritative condemnations of the modernist impulse in contemporary theology. Appearing in 1907, Pope Pius X's decree *Lamentabili* and his encyclical *Pascendi* spelled out the church's absolute opposition to any theological project of mediation attempting to reconcile Catholic belief with modern thought. Continuing a line of papal teaching beginning with Gregory XVI's *Mirari vos* (1832) and Pius IX's *Quanta cura* (1864), the twentieth-century documents defined modernism as "the synthesis of all heresies."[8] With the subsequent imposition of the Anti-Modernist Oath in 1910, requiring the subject to swear fidelity to the "*certain* charism of *truth*" in the church's deposit of faith, the Catholic Church laid clear restrictions limiting the intellectual activity of priests and professors in Catholic universities.[9] Pius X's successor, Benedict XV, reaffirmed the condemnation of modernism in his plea for world peace, *Ad beatissimi apostolorum* (1914), and in 1922 Pius XI expanded the meaning of the controversial term to include "a species of moral, legal, and social modernism which We condemn, no less decidedly than We condemn theological modernism."[10]

Much has been written on the condition of Catholic intellectual life after the promulgation of these documents.[11] Often historians have referred to the "fortress" or "siege" mentality that characterized Roman Catholic thought in the aftermath of the modernist crisis.[12] Concentrating on the restraints placed upon the education of priests, these studies have correctly noted the parochial character of the period's seminary education, the "intellectual slumber" of Catholic scholarly journals, and the failure of Catholic universities to achieve reputations as scholarly research institutions.[13] Likewise, studies focusing on the Vatican's control of clerical life, its censorship of theological writings, and its organization of vigilance committees to ferret out suspected modernists have typically characterized Rome's administrative effort to identify and discipline modernist theologians as a repressive trend within Catholic intellectual life—a "witch hunt" or an "inquisitorial reign of terror," devastating Catholic intellectual life for at least a generation.[14]

Contrary to the standard interpretation, however, the official anti-modernism of the church did not inaugurate a totally stagnant period in Catholic thought. As historian James Hitchcock has observed, the caricature of early twentieth-century Catholic thought as timid and inane fails to reckon with the significant number of unbelieving intellectual elites who were drawn to the Catholic faith during the antimodernist episode in church history.[15] In fact, most of the leading converts of the Catholic Revival entered the church only *after* the 1907 condemnation of modernism. In England, for example, historian Christopher Dawson converted in 1914, Anglican chaplain Ronald Knox embraced the faith in 1917, and Chesterton entered the Roman Catholic Church in 1922.

Rejecting the strategy of liberal Protestantism designed to attract Christianity's "cultured despisers" by minimizing claims to infallible truth and reliance upon a supernatural world view, the intellectual converts to Catholicism overcame long-standing cultural barriers to accept the Catholic religion precisely because of its claim to possess a body of supernaturally revealed dogma.[16] They were not inspired by a demythologized Christianity, nor were they convinced of the apologetic potential of the modernist project. As Ronald Knox put it, "the latitudinarian appeal, as a matter of experience, does not attract."[17] Rather, like Chesterton, the Revival converts found the church's insistence upon doctrinal accuracy curiously "romantic." Regularly, they described submission of the intellect to the mind of the church as an act of "mental emancipation."[18] Thomas Merton, for instance, thought it a liberating thing "to breathe the clean atmosphere of orthodox tradition."[19] Seeing themselves as spiritual heirs to Newman's opposition to nineteenth-century liberalism, the intellectuals of the twentieth-century Catholic Revival were stimulated, not stifled, by the church's critique of modernity.

There are many examples of this phenomenon in early twentieth-century Catholic thought. Jacques Maritain's nearly fifteen-year association with the illiberal Action Française movement provides an intriguing instance. While often treated by admirers of the French Thomist as an embarrassing episode in the philosopher's life, it is now recognized as more than the misguided right-wing backlash of a naive convert. As John Hellman has shown, the celebrated theocentric humanism articulated in Maritain's mature work "was inspired by hostility to the modern world."[20] *Antimoderne*, the convert's 1922 publication, was followed by a stinging rejection of modern thought in *Three Reformers* (1925) and a dire prediction of Western culture's collapse in *The Twilight of Civilization* (1939).[21] Tying the problems of modern society directly to the "dissolution of Christendom," Maritain made his antimodernist convictions particularly clear in *True Humanism* (1936):

> The condemnation which [the Christian] pronounces on modern civilisation is indeed more grave and more reasoned than that of the socialist or the communist, since it is not only the terrestrial happiness of the community, it is also the life of the soul and the person's spiritual destiny that are menaced by this civilisation.[22]

In similar fashion, Christopher Dawson linked his hope for "a restoration of Christian order" to his unbending critique of the West's departure from the moral unity of an earlier Christian culture. His faith in the Western humanist tradition derived not from his confidence in the progress of culture but rather from a gloomy prophecy of Europe's post-Catholic future. Wary of the new political "Leviathan" created by a secularized West cut off from its spiritual roots, he could not imagine a truly democratic society detached from traditional Christian values. He even defended Pius IX's infamous *Syllabus of Errors*, because, in his opinion, modern secular liberalism denied "the subordination of human society to divine law."[23] American proponents of the Revival, too, founded the dream of a re-Christianized world on frankly antimodernist premises. Jesuit educator Calvert Alexander, who dubbed contemporary Catholic writing "a literature of protest" against the post-Renaissance West, marshaled evidence in *The Catholic*

Literary Revival to show that a revived Christian civilization would emerge only from the "double collapse of Protestantism and the dreams of the Science and Progress cult."[24]

Corresponding to this critique of modernity was the Revival's marked admiration for the Middle Ages. For many Revival enthusiasts, particularly those engaged in programs of Catholic Action, a warmly imaginative medievalism helped to humanize an otherwise cranky anti-modernism.[25] During the Catholic Revival of the nineteenth century, a number of forces, from the circulation of Walter Scott novels to the practice of bourgeois antiquarianism, conspired to reinforce the centrality of the Middle Ages in the European Christian conscience. British literary critic Matthew Arnold, suspicious of the fashions driving Victorian tastes, suggested that Newman's Catholic solution to the perplexing problems of the modern mind might be attributed to "the last enchantments of the Middle Age."[26] Later, capitalizing on the nineteenth century's interest in things medieval, Chesterton developed a contagiously positive image of the era in his popular biographies of medieval saints Francis of Assisi and Thomas Aquinas. Polemical writers like Hilaire Belloc laced their histories of Europe with apologies for feudal institutions, and uncritical survey texts like James J. Walsh's *The Thirteenth, Greatest of Centuries* (1907) became standard fare in Catholic schools for decades. Catholic novelists, for their part, captured the mystery of medieval spirituality in fiction. Achieving a high level of intellectual artistry, Norway's Nobel Prize winner, Sigrid Undset, intrigued an international audience of readers with the saga of *Kristin Lavransdatter* set in medieval Scandinavia.

While critics of the Revival charged such literature with distorting actual history, Jacques Maritain attempted to establish the movement's attachment to the medieval period on philosophical grounds. For him, the Revival's elevation of the Middle Ages was not an exercise in nostalgic romance, but the isolation of a "*concrete historical ideal*" for a new Christendom. Understanding "Christendom" to mean a "*temporal* regime whose formations, in very varying degrees and in very varying ways, bear the stamp of the christian conception of life," Maritain used the medieval period as a conceptual model to clarify the shape of a re-Christianized culture in modern pluralistic society. Counting the ancient and medieval periods as the two major epochs of Christian growth and maturity, he assigned to modernity a purely negative role in salvation history. The era of the Christian "diaspora," it functioned in his historical scheme as a mere "parenthesis" between medieval Christendom and the imminent dispensation of a renewed Christendom. He expressed the positive side of the Catholic Revival's antimodernism when he dreamed of a "third age" in Western history, which would "save among the broken forms of history the imperishable substance of the past, and above all of the christian past of Europe, in the elaboration of a christian historical ideal capable of existence and inviting realisation under a new historic sky."[27]

Schola Prophetarum

Addressing an audience at Windsor, Ontario's Assumption University in 1958, just a few months before the election of John XXIII and the announcement of a new ecumenical council, Allen Tate displayed his sympathies for this aspect of the Catholic Revival when he spoke with guarded optimism of his hope for "the reappearance of a Catholic intelligence which flourished in the three centuries from about the year 1100."[28] Like Maritain, he invested medieval society with paradigmatic status and appropriated from it criteria for the criticism of modern culture. Though he repeatedly denied that his admiration for the Middle Ages entailed reversion to an ideal past, he shared the Catholic Revival's affection for the period and used it as the reference point for discussion of a restored Christian civilization. The organic unity of the culture, the agrarian pattern of its economy, and the common mythic structure shaping its vision were stock features of the Revival's interpretation of the Middle Ages, but they appealed to the same instincts in Tate that drove him to reject much of what he found mediocre and destabilizing in modern culture. For most of his career, Dante figured as the icon of the fully developed artist in Christian society, and the medieval university served as his model for the understanding of genuine religious humanism.

In hindsight, it is easy to see how Tate, trained in a southern classical tradition more at home in the nineteenth century than the twentieth, came to accept the classicism of preconciliar Catholic thought as a refreshing alternative to the intellectual offerings of modernity. When he first considered the value of Roman Catholicism, antimodernism was central to the church's thought and apologetic mission. More than any other theme, it was Catholic opposition to modernity that resonated with his emerging views of culture. In fact, he initially developed an appreciation for Catholicism as an extension of his own misgivings about modernity. Tate, however, approached Catholicism by a singularly indirect route. Except for the classical pattern of his education and a year at a Catholic preparatory school that may have disposed him favorably toward the Catholic intellectual tradition, there was little in his background that prepared him for a career as a Catholic antimodernist.

Though an acquired hostility to modernity eventually paved the way for Tate's acceptance of Catholicism, his was a tortured path.

Raised in a home virtually devoid of religious instruction, Tate and his two older brothers gained only a vague sense of religious identity from their father, an inactive member of the Episcopal Church whom Allen called a "Robert S. Ingersoll Free Thinker." Tate's mother, the "puritanical" daughter of a "lapsed, but not apostate" Catholic and his Calvinistic wife, halfheartedly encouraged attendance at Presbyterian Sunday school and severely banned card-playing in the home. She had little sense of faith beyond the level of conventional Christian sympathies. "In so far as we had a family religion," Tate wrote, "it was my mother's, and it was less Christian in daily practice than Chinese; for she worshiped her father and by a kind of genealogical sorites arrived at the veneration of remote, invisible forbears."[29]

Due to a mysterious scandal repressed in family memory for years, Tate's father lived apart from his family and withdrew from social life when Allen was still a young boy. After the separation of his parents, Tate's youth involved brief sojourns in a number of locations across the upper South, interspersed with summer visits to relations in tidewater Virginia and the area around Washington, D.C. "Until I was thirty," he said, "I never lived in one place longer than three years."[30] Shuttled back and forth between the cities of the Ohio Valley, Tate attended several schools, public and private, receiving an erratic education that enhanced his childhood bent toward literature but left him deficient in mathematics and related subjects.

After a disappointing year at the Cincinnati Conservatory of Music, during which he dreamed of pursuing a career as a concert violinist, his mother enrolled him in the Jesuit-run Georgetown Preparatory School outside of Baltimore, where his Catholic grandfather had studied before the Civil War. There he submitted to the demands of a classical curriculum that still retained the shape of the *trivium* and *quadrivium*, the medieval liberal arts. At least one biographical sketch, written for the school's alumni magazine, has speculated that Tate's year in the "Jesuit stability" of the institution may have "planted a spiritual seed" in his consciousness.[31]

Whatever the long-term spiritual consequences of his year in Catholic prep school, Tate's experience at Georgetown made little impact on his immediate set of loyalties and aspirations. In fact, by the time he matriculated at Vanderbilt University in 1918, the trajectory of his intellectual life was already aimed away from the South's classical tradition. Though he excelled in Greek and Latin composition, in the study of oriental languages, and in his knowledge of the ancient dramatists, poets, and historians, other factors besides his classical education profoundly influenced the course of Tate's intellectual life during his years at Vanderbilt.

In the 1920s, Nashville's Vanderbilt University was hardly the place for the training of a future antimodernist. In fact, in the previous decade the populist-turned-fundamentalist William Jennings Bryan denounced it as "the center of Modernism in the South."[32] Recently free from the oversight of the bishops of the Methodist Episcopal Church, South, the university's administration, led by their progressive chancellor James H. Kirkland, anxiously sought to make the school an example of advanced, non-sectarian higher education. With painful reminders of Reconstruction-era poverty and provincialism still surrounding them, they traded upon Nashville's growing reputation as the "Athens of the South" and wed Vanderbilt to the aims and values of the bustling New South. Sharing the concerns of the civic boosters on the local Chamber of Commerce, Vanderbilt's administrators hoped to divest themselves of the regional hostilities and peculiarities of the South of the Lost Cause in order to enjoy the blessings of a belated "gilded age" of southern economic prosperity and social improvement. They dreamed of making their institution a cultural showpiece in an urbanized and industrialized South, transformed by commercial success. Though they bristled under the acerbic sarcasm of H. L. Mencken's infamous critique of the South, they reluctantly agreed with the particulars of the fellow southerner's caustic essay, "Sahara of the Bozart" (1917): the South as a whole must engage in progressive uplift if it is ever to shuck its stereotype as America's cultural backwater.[33]

As a college undergraduate, Tate gained a reputation on the Vanderbilt campus as a precocious young artist, eager to leave behind the burden of the benighted South. Living in Wesley Hall, the university's old theology building designed in a "Methodist Gothic" style, he took pleasure in positioning himself beyond the reaches of conventional southern piety, describing himself once as an "enforced atheist."[34] He was even known to walk the Nashville campus mischievously sporting a copy of Mencken under his arm. Tate's first mentor, literature professor John Crowe Ransom, once confided in his student, venturing the opinion that "for you and me and the elite whom I know—art is the true religion and no other is needed."[35] Years later, Tate confirmed this conclusion regarding the worldly spirituality of his college years. "A young man furnished by his literary environment with a literary religion," he said, "could not be concerned with theological salvation."[36] At the time, the young Tate proudly declared his "tendency to sympathize with almost anything revolutionary, sensible or not, and at the same time to derogate conservatism of all kinds."[37]

A significant part of Tate's collegiate experience was his involvement in the local Fugitive poetry group. Composed of a small cluster of professional and amateur writers associated with the Vanderbilt community, the Fugitives met informally in private homes for the reading and criticism of original literary works. From 1922 to 1925, with the financial backing of Nashville businessmen, they published a literary magazine called the *Fugitive*, which historians have credited with launching the first phase of the Southern Literary Renaissance.[38] When Tate joined the group in 1921, Ransom and his junior colleague on the English faculty, Donald Davidson, were emerging as the true intellectual leaders of the group. Other members included Merrill Moore, Jesse Wills, Alec Brock Stevenson, and Tate's roommate Robert Penn Warren. The moderator of the Fugitives' meetings, Sidney Mttron Hirsch, an eccentric Jew addressed as "Doctor" despite his lack of academic degree, animated the sessions with a "vast, if somewhat perverse, erudition" and an overactive Rosicrucian imagination.[39]

Like the Inklings in Britain, the Oxford writers surrounding C. S. Lewis and J. R. R. Tolkien during the 1930s, the Fugitive circle was an all male group of writers dedicated to nurturing artistic creativity through collegial criticism.[40] In contrast to the Inklings, whose conversations exhibited the typically English reticence regarding religion,[41] the Fugitives relished discussions of what they vaguely called "philosophy." Formal studies of the Fugitive group have tended to emphasize the members' contributions to the South's literary culture, often obscuring the acute interest of the initial participants in the intellectually fashionable subjects of Asian religions, esoteric theosophy, Jewish mysticism, and biblical criticism. The *Fugitive*'s announcement that "THE FUGITIVE flees from nothing faster than from the high-caste Brahmins of the Old South"[42] revealed not only the group's well-known departure from the "genteel tradition" of southern literary discourse, but also their fascination with religious options at odds with twentieth-century American orthodoxy.

"The Right Kind of Modernism"

In spite of their intellectual curiosity, Tate thought his fellow Fugitives hopelessly old-fashioned, impatient with the cultural mediocrity of the New South but "trapped in the middle-class manners of Nashville."[43] As the first undergraduate member of the Fugitives, he tried to introduce his colleagues to the new movement of literary modernism then gaining notoriety among critics in touch with the "lost-generation" communities of expatriate American writers in postwar London and Paris. Looking back on the period, Ransom noted that Tate possessed "literary resources which were not the property of our region at that time." Tate wrote, he said, "in the consciousness of a body of literature which was unknown to his fellow students, and to my faculty associates and myself."[44]

Enthralled with the work of expatriate T. S. Eliot, Tate spearheaded the southern revolt against Victorian poetic sentiment. The modernism of Eliot convinced him that the Fugitive rejection of the local color legacy of polite southern letters was simply one shot in an irrepressible literary civil war already underway. Influenced by Eliot's poetry, especially the intellectual autonomy and technical virtuosity in *The Waste Land* (1922), Tate, advocating bold and unrestricted experimentation in literary form, mystified his colleagues with his "extremely unusual" contributions to the *Fugitive*.[45] Ransom, engaged in public and sometimes painful debate with Tate on the value of Eliot's work, warned his student "against going to extreme lengths in modernism."[46]

At the same time that Tate began to appropriate the technique and spirit of the modernist style, he also began to display keen interest in the peculiar intellectual complexities of Eliot's brand of modernism—a modernism with deep reservations about modernity. As a response to the horror and brutality of the First World War, the modernist impulse that Tate found so intriguing represented more than a bohemian rebellion against bourgeois manners and literary custom. Modernism also contained a curiously traditionalist strain of commentary on the modern situation.

The Sacred Wood (1920), Eliot's first major contribution to literary criticism, inspired Tate to embark on what amounted to a lifelong crusade against the Emersonian-Whitmanian cult of expressionism in literature—the popular notion that art is the expression of an artist's emotions. In that volume, Eliot's landmark essay, "Tradition and the Individual Talent" (1919), privileged the place of living tradition in the mental world of the artist and indicted the nineteenth-century heritage for privatizing art's function in an ahistorical conception of society. Paralleling the work of British critics T. E. Hulme and I. A. Richards, the essay articulated an "impersonal" theory of literature that ran counter to the subjectivism of the prevailing romantic attitude toward aesthetic creativity. For Eliot, poetry meant "not a turning loose of emotion, but an escape from emotion." The authentic creation of art, he maintained, entails the "continual extinction of personality" in the poet, who is conscious "not only of the pastness of the past, but of its presence."[47]

This new emphasis on classical formalism, opposed to the modern premium set upon originality and self-expression, carried distinctly social overtones. The recovery of tradition in aesthetic theory matched a search for hierarchy and order in the chaotic modern social realm. Some literary modernists, repulsed by what George Orwell called "the ugliness and spiritual emptiness of the machine age,"[48] looked to the classicism of premodern social institutions for redemptive solutions to the problems in modern Western nations. Shocked by the moral bankruptcy of wartime Europe, they employed a mythology of historical decline to mix their *avant-garde* poetics with a resurgence of right-wing political conservatism. Finding the modern world hopelessly bleak and decadent, they sought amid the ruins of the modern West materials with which to reconstruct a reliable cultural tradition. Some, like Vorticist writer Wyndham Lewis and Imagist poet Ezra Pound, balanced their modernist aesthetic tastes with well-publicized fascist convictions in the political arena. To them, Hitler and Mussolini represented plausible answers to the problems of modernity.[49] Others, like Hulme and Eliot, expressed admiration for the restoration of crown and altar proposed by the leader of Action Française, French traditionalist Charles Maurras.[50] Eliot's antimodernism eventually led him to reject the legacy of his family's liberal Unitarianism as well as his American citizenship. By 1928, he declared himself "classicist in literature, royalist in politics, and anglo-catholic in religion."[51] In *After Strange Gods: A Primer of Modern Heresy* (1933), infamous for its remarks on the deleterious effects of "free-thinking Jews" in Western society, he diagnosed modern culture as "worm-eaten with Liberalism."[52] Only a reinvigorated Christian culture, he said, could "save the World from Suicide."[53]

In a recent study of Tate's modernism, Langdon Hammer has offered a critical re-examination of the double-edged quality of modernism. According to Hammer, modernism contained two contrasting impulses: one, reactionary, elitist, antifeminist, and homophobic; the other, revolutionary, democratizing, feminist, and homoerotic. In his early verse and critical work, Tate exhibited both sides of this "Janus-faced" modernist vision.[54] He juggled a revolt against Victorian aesthetic moralism with contempt for the conventions of modern progressive thought. Like Eliot, he gradually earned a dual reputation among "lost-generation" intellectuals. On the one hand, he was a prime American architect of the modernist period style—what many considered a risky departure from the canons of literary propriety. On the other, he was becoming a leading figure in the interwar resurgence of American conservatism—what

William Barrett referred to as the "Counter-Enlightenment."[55] Joining in the cultural polemics of the period, Tate identified the reactionary rejection of modernity as "the right kind of modernism."[56]

According to Albert J. Montesi, Tate revealed the influence of Eliot more than any other American writer of the generation.[57] In a letter of 1925, Tate confessed that Eliot "writes up my own ideas much better than my poor skill permits me to do for myself."[58] The extent of Eliot's influence upon him was especially clear in Tate's readiness to link his work in literature to larger programs of cultural criticism, particularly those incorporating religious criticism. As Eliot put it, "Literary criticism should be completed by criticism from a definite ethical and theological standpoint."[59] In spite of his admiration for Eliot, however, Tate clearly demonstrated an initial reluctance to follow his mentor into the Anglican Church or any other church. Fellow Fugitive Donald Davidson warned him not to "give up the ghost in favor of a combination of classic-Anglo-Catholic-Conservative" ideologies.[60] Always wary of Anglophilia, Tate was not even tempted. In fact, before he turned to Roman Catholicism as a medium for his antimodernist critique, Tate invested his energies in a project of religious criticism the particularities of which Eliot could never have endorsed. As a leader in the Southern Agrarian movement of the late 1920s and early 1930s, Tate began his long career as religious critic in response to an event that reawakened his southern identity and that of his closest colleagues. An unlikely commencement for a career in Catholic criticism, the 1925 trial of John T. Scopes for teaching evolution in a Tennessee public school afforded Tate his first opportunity to exercise his newfound antimodernism in the context of religious debate.

"Like a Midnight Alarm"

The significance of Southern Agrarianism has long been documented by literary and intellectual histories of the twentieth-century South.[61] Drawing upon themes in the larger American canon of pastoral anti-urbanism and independent regionalism, the movement represented one distinctive voice among a chorus of dissident voices calling into question the assumptions driving the modernization of American society in the early decades of the twentieth century.[62] Evolving out of the Fugitive group, what came to be known as the Southern Agrarian "symposium" engaged Tate and his fellow Nashville writers in an unusual project of social criticism after the *Fugitive* ceased publication in 1925. The symposium, comprising twelve men representing a variety of artistic and academic pursuits, including literature, psychology, history, and theater, had at its core Tate and the other chief Fugitives, Ransom and Davidson. Though they remained relatively alienated from the temperament of Tate's literary modernism, the former Fugitives did share Tate's growing dissatisfaction with aspects of postwar American culture. Known as the Agrarians because of their aggressive opposition to the mass-culture of modern America, they isolated industrialism as the key feature of a social economy jeopardizing the survival of traditional patterns of art, education, politics, and other cultural folkways.

In the heyday of the movement, all of the Agrarians identified religion as a crucial issue in their analysis of modern culture. In individual works and collaborative efforts, such as the Agrarian "manifesto" *I'll Take My Stand: The South and the Agrarian Tradition* (1930) and its sequel *Who Owns America?* (1936),[63] they attacked not only the industrialism of the northern capitalist and the New South booster, but also "the spiritual poverty that marks the age of machines."[64] An early student of the movement, Virginia Rock, wrote: "Religion—or at least an awareness of and respect for the power and mystery of the supernatural—was fundamental in Agrarianism."[65] Viewing the economic structure of society as "the secular image of religion," and religion as the "background of metaphysical doctrine which dictates [a society's] political economy," the Agrarians felt compelled to drive their critique of modernity beyond the conventional contrast of the virtues of an agricultural economy with the vices of an industrial system.[66] They insisted that the heart of the matter was not merely the economic arrangement of modern culture, but the religious faith, or absence of faith, informing the culture as a whole.

Historians of Southern Agrarianism have frequently identified 1925 as the *annus mirabilis* of the movement.[67] Though analysis of the correspondence among the principal Agrarians shows that plans for a southern symposium did not begin to take shape until 1927 or 1928,[68] the Agrarians themselves in later years often pointed to the 1925 Scopes trial as a key event which triggered the transformation of a bookish circle of poets into a band of defiant apologists for southern tradition. At the 1956 reunion of the Fugitive poets, the surviving Agrarians traced the first stirrings of the movement to the time "when the Dayton trial set everything aflame."[69] In lectures at Georgia's Mercer University the following year, Donald Davidson testified to the spiritual significance of the "Dayton unpleasantness" in the development of the Agrarian consciousness. "With its jeering accompaniment of large-scale mockery directed against Tennessee and the South," he said, the Scopes trial "broke in upon our literary concerns like a midnight alarm."[70]

Curiously, during the most intense phase of their activity, a number of the Agrarian critics, including Tate, built into their rhetorical strategies the imaginative use of a new term popularized by American journalists during the controversial trial. The Agrarians chose the new religious movement of fundamentalism as the religious symbol to embody their critique of modernity. Despite the fact that the main exponents of Agrarianism were generally unaffiliated with traditional Protestantism (and some were openly hostile to organized religion), the Agrarian movement recognized fundamentalism as a powerful mode of protest against oppressive currents in modern culture. While rejecting the world view of theistic supernaturalism, they nevertheless admitted that the fundamentalist objection to the cherished assumptions of modern America possessed a measure of moral validity. Like other secular "Young Intellectuals" of the 1920s, upset with narrow-minded American progressivism, the Agrarians advanced unique arguments for fundamentalism on humanistic grounds.[71]

Originally coined by Baptist editor Curtis Lee Laws in 1920 to designate the conservative party among northern Protestants, the term "fundamentalism" quickly became a pejorative term in the popular American lexicon. Suggesting the homemade theology of itinerant tent revivalists, the emotional excesses of under-educated "holy rollers," and the crazed rituals of fanatic snake-handlers, the term came to represent for many Americans traditional folk religion's radical incompatibility with modernity. Astute scholars such as H. Richard Niebuhr bought the wholesale identification of fundamentalism with unsophisticated rural faith and frontier piety.[72] Ironically unaware of the northern and urban origins of fundamentalism now well known to historians of the movement,[73] even the Agrarians themselves blindly accepted the harsh and often inaccurate stereotype of fundamentalism advanced by early-twentieth-century opponents of conservative Protestantism. However, unlike nervous southern progressives, including the administration of Vanderbilt University, who frantically tried to refute the stubborn stereotype and dissociate fundamentalism from southern culture, the Agrarians appropriated "fundamentalism" precisely in the terms of its detractors. Transforming it into an instrument of counterattack, they introduced "fundamentalism" into their discourse as a charged synecdoche signifying those aspects of traditional humane culture that they thought threatened by a contemporary wave of intellectual intolerance. Much as a poet takes on a fictive persona in the creation of lyric verse, the Agrarians borrowed the alien voice of fundamentalism in polemical prose to express their antimodern social criticism. Confirming George Marsden's suspicion that southern writers of the interwar period shared fundamentalists' sense of alienation from mainstream American culture, the Agrarian use of fundamentalism reflects the deliberate attempt of "lost-generation" critics of modernity to foster an intellectual affinity with the ultimate outsiders in early-twentieth-century America—those R. Laurence Moore has provocatively dubbed "America's other Lost Generation."[74] Far from a sign of reproach, "fundamentalism" became for the Agrarians a flexible signifier in their quarrel with modernity.

Convinced that the condescending attitude of America's intellectuals toward conservative southern evangelicals was only one aspect of a massive program of cultural imperialism, a "cold Civil War" in other words, Donald Davidson employed fundamentalism as a token of devout resistance to dangerous nationwide trends toward cultural standardization.[75] His first published reference to fundamentalism dealt with what would become a conventional Agrarian theme: the southern writer's need for a living local tradition to nourish art. Neither the "moonlight and magnolias" legacy of Old South sentimentalism nor the trite civic optimism of New South commercialism, Davidson declared, could furnish the arts with a proper environment in which to thrive. Consequently, he pictured the southern artist as "an alien particle in the body politic." At the same time, however, he suggested that the artist's salvation may lie in the dialectical acceptance of the culture's meager resources. For Davidson, the religion of the Dayton anti-evolutionists became a figure for what Mencken's "benighted" South could grant the artist:

> Fundamentalism, in one aspect, is blind and belligerent ignorance; in another, it represents a fierce clinging to poetic supernaturalism against the encroachments of cold logic; it stands for moral seriousness. The Southerner should hesitate to scorn these qualities, for, however much they may now be perverted to bigoted and unfruitful uses, they belong in the bone and sinew of his nature as they once belonged to Milton, who was both Puritan and Cavalier. To obscure them by a show of sophistication is to play the coward; to give them a positive transmutation is the highest function of art.[76]

Treating fundamentalism as a native folk art, Davidson asserted the value of indigenous culture, whatever its limitations. As other southerners would turn the humiliation of past defeat into a glorious Lost Cause, modeled in part on the Miltonic theodicy of failed English Puritanism, he grasped the alleged backwardness of fundamentalism as a rugged virtue by which the remnants of stable local culture in America could shield themselves from the mass-produced culture of the age. In the same way that southern-born fundamentalist theologian J. Gresham Machen feared modern democracy's power to "make of America one huge 'Main Street,' where spiritual adventure will be discouraged,"[77] Davidson used "fundamentalism" as a timely witness against the leveling of the American cultural landscape.[78]

Likewise, the Agrarian writer Stark Young, when confronted with the truncated Christianity of progressive middle-class businessmen, announced his preference for "a certain rude reality in the Southern drift toward religion."[79] Another outspoken Agrarian, Andrew Lytle, wary of social pressures toward ideological conformity, advised his fellow southerners to "turn away the liberal capons who fill the pulpits" and seek preachers bold enough "to renounce science and search out the Word in the authorities." In his essay, "The Hind Tit," Lytle summed up much of the Agrarian spirit: "If we have to spit in the water-bucket to keep it our own, we had better do it."[80]

At the Fugitives' reunion in 1956, Davidson allowed that the Agrarian symposium was as much "a defense of poetry" as a defense of southern culture.[81] Though a sentiment shared by all the original participants, it was John Crowe Ransom who gave the theme its unique place in the Agrarian philosophy. Concerned like his Agrarian brethren to make the world safe for southern farmers, Ransom, the son of a Methodist minister, aligned himself with his fundamentalist contemporaries to ensure the survival of poets as well. While his department chairman scrambled to publish his upbeat book on *The Advancing South* (1926) and Vanderbilt's chancellor announced plans for a progressive School of Religion to counter "belligerent fundamentalism,"[82] Ransom was agitated by what he saw as an encroaching positivism overtaking the academy and the American mind. Though he came to reject the traditional Christian faith of his father, he exploited "fundamentalism" in his defense of the rights of poetic imagination against the myopia of what he called chauvinistic "scientism."[83]

Ransom's 1930 text, *God Without Thunder: An Unorthodox Defense of Orthodoxy*, advanced his reflections on the "psychic necessity" of religious supernaturalism. Couched in the context of a highly speculative account of the secularization of Western religion, the book's central argument amounted to an explanation of religion similar to the aesthetic theory of religion developed by naturalist philosopher George Santayana. According to Santayana, Harvard's famous "Catholic atheist," religion functions in culture as a great poem. With a mysterious power foreign to the discursive reason of science, its "fictions" communicate the pathos and nobility of human life.[84] Like Santayana, whose works he read throughout the 1920s and 1930s, Ransom maintained that religion was a species of poetry, inescapably tied to tropes and figures resisting rationalization. Though he denied them any claim to verifiable truth, he granted the myths of Christian supernaturalism an integral function in the essential nature of the religion—so much so that, as he saw it, being religious was tantamount to being orthodox. For this reason, while he judged them analogous to Kant's "necessary fictions," Ransom nevertheless held that religious myths "attempt to express truths which are not accessible to science."[85] Though they do not correspond to empirical reality, he said, the myths and symbols of religion are critical components of a healthy civilization.

As William Shea has observed, Santayana, like Freud and other modern critics of religion, preferred "the errors of religious orthodoxy" to the rational reinterpretations of religion set forth by modernist theologians busy attempting to salvage religious belief for the modern mind.[86] Without supernatural myth, Santayana said, religion ceases to be a living reality. Modernism, a poor substitute for living religion, represents religion shorn of its most interesting qualities. Concentrating on his native Catholicism, he said, "The supernaturalism, the literal realism, the other-worldliness of the Catholic church are too much the soul of it to depart without causing its dissolution." To illustrate his idiosyncratic theory of religion, Santayana surmised that antimodernist Pope Pius X represented one of the modern world's last practitioners of true religion.[87] Ransom, for his part, accorded the honor to the Protestant fundamentalists of Dayton, Tennessee. "My own view," he said, "is that all first-class religionists are Fundamentalists, and that it is the Fundamentalists, properly speaking, who constitute the Church." Ransom praised fundamentalists for regarding "their God as an actuality" and treating "their supernatural fictions as natural objects," just as the patriot "caught in the act of saluting a striped rag does not feel obliged to stop and offer the qualification that he honors it only as the symbol of something else." In contrast to Christian modernists, whose higher criticism feared "the vigorous detail of the concrete myth," and to "Gnostic" readers of Sir James Frazer's *Golden Bough*, whose cultural relativism promiscuously embraced all myths, Ransom's fundamentalists instinctively recognized the poetic principle that "myths do not work in human civilization except when they are dogmas, tolerably hard, and exceedingly jealous of their rivals." Ransom's *God Without Thunder* diagnosed in modern science and its theological admirers "a defect of the poetic temperament."[88]

"To Make a World, or Bring Back One"

Tate was perhaps the least likely member of the Fugitive-Agrarian circle to espouse pro-fundamentalist rhetoric in a critique of secular culture. After graduation from Vanderbilt in 1923, his life conformed to the pattern outlined in Malcolm Cowley's *Exile's Return* (1934), the classic history of America's literary "lost generation."[89] Departing the South to launch an ambitious free-lance writing career, he spent the rest of the decade in the countercultural communities fostering that generation of artists. In New York's Greenwich Village, he associated with writers such as Cowley, Hart Crane, Edmund Wilson, and Ford Maddox Ford. Later, in Paris, he joined the "*petit cercle*" of Left Bank expatriates Gertrude Stein, Ernest Hemingway, Sylvia Beach, and F. Scott Fitzgerald. He also met and married the aspiring southern novelist Carolyn (later Caroline) Gordon.[90]

At first, Tate was eager to put the South behind him. Still agreeing with Mencken's indictment of the South's cultural barrenness, he wrote a piece for the *Nation*, in which he decried his region for its determination to be "a One-hoss Shay forever."[91] By his own confession, he was "sort of disgusted with the South."[92] In time, however, Tate began to reevaluate the sources of his identity and reconsider his relationship to the South. Later, reflecting on these years, he said, "I began to feel that we had something [in the South], after all, that I shouldn't let go of."[93] By the end of 1925, Tate was immersed in the study of antebellum southern history and the genealogical history of his own family. According to Andrew Lytle, whom Tate met in New York City, animated discussions of the Scopes trial sparked the dramatic shift in Tate's thought.[94] The next year he commenced work on what would become his best known poetic work, "Ode to the Confederate Dead." Increasingly he looked to his southern heritage for traditional resources to resist the meaninglessness he found in modernity. He "became a Southerner again," he said, by leaving the South.[95]

Tate entered the larger American literary culture during the great period of American expatriation—cultural and geographical. As exile from their seemingly provincial country led many of his contemporaries to a new appreciation for what one of their generation, literary historian Perry Miller, habitually called "the meaning of America," Tate's absence from the South offered in a similar way an unexpected occasion to reconsider the resources of his region's heritage, especially its religious culture. Compounded by the combination of Mencken's attack on southern culture and the ridicule heaped upon the South after the Scopes trial, Tate's expatriate experience served to reinforce within him a distinctively sectional consciousness. With the "backward glance" that he later identified as the origin of the South's literary renaissance, Tate, like the speaker in his "Ode to the Confederate Dead," turned his "eyes to the immoderate past."[96]

As letters passed across the Atlantic, back and forth between Tate and the former Fugitives, the idea for a southern "symposium" preoccupied Tate. Once committed to the Agrarian cause, he focused on religion as the key issue in his critique of modern society. Early in the deliberations, however, he sought to make distinctions between his positions and those of his colleagues. Convinced that Agrarianism should exceed Davidson's defensive plea for southern uniqueness, Tate advocated a strategic "return to the provinces," southern and otherwise, to promote the ideal of traditional society founded on a common religion.[97] Also aware of the limitations of Ransom's aesthetic theory of religion, he laced his early Agrarianism with arguments for the necessity of a particular, historic religion supporting the totality of culture. Consequently, Tate, like his fellow Agrarians, drew upon the animus of fundamentalism to bolster his Agrarian discourse. Yet he did so in a strangely cosmopolitan way. Using the symbol of obstinate fundamentalism as a heuristic device, he attempted to address not only the South's social dilemma, but also the nagging problem of the spiritual condition of Western culture as a whole.

Even in his earliest works published during college, Tate was asking, "Whom and what shall our souls believe?"[98] Like Eliot, he realized that his incapacity for satisfying religious belief was symptomatic of a widespread malaise among moderns. In the *Fugitive* he wrote, "An individualistic intellectualism is the mood of our age. There is no common-to-all-truth....Our time cleaves to no racial myth."[99] Repeatedly Dante and Milton figured in his writings as painful reminders of the modern West's lack of a coherent mythic structure shaping its thought and art. Echoing Eliot's concern regarding the modern writer's alienation from tradition, he said, "I am convinced that Milton himself could not write a Paradise Lost now. Minds are less important for literature than culture; our minds are as good as they were, but our culture is dissolving."[100] Similarly, in the *New Republic*, he wrote: "The advantages the poet had in Dante's time are obvious: his chief interest focused on his method, the ordered differentiation of his perceptions within a given scheme. The modern poet has to construct, besides his personal vision, the scheme itself."[101] Gravitating into the orbit of an international community of modern mandarins yielding what Marshall Berman called an aesthetics of cultural despair,[102] Tate interpreted the disintegration of the European Christian "scheme" as disastrous for all aspects of cultural life. Believing that rampant naturalism was sabotaging the Western intellectual tradition, he wondered if society could survive the demise of its traditional myths and beliefs. In order to enjoy a culture founded on a sense of enduring faith, Tate concluded, "we have got to make a world, or bring back one, whose conditions of being make it possible."[103]

What Robert Dupree has referred to as Tate's "fundamentalist project"[104] began as he contemplated the moral barriers to the creation or retrieval of such a world. His 1926 review of Spengler's *The Decline of the West*, appearing under the provocative title "Fundamentalism," revealed to progressive readers of the *Nation* Tate's agreement with the German intellectual's pessimistic philosophy of history. Indeed, he found in Spengler's rejection of progress and his distrust of scientific-commercial society fashionable academic support for his reactionary approach to culture.[105] Like classical Tiresias, Eliot's prophet of doom in *The Waste Land*, Tate stained his criticism with a dark vision of the breakdown of Western civilization.

At the same time, Tate was making preparations for a monograph on the conflict between science and religion. Describing plans for an essay on fundamentalism—"not what the Methodist Bishops think it is, but what it really is"—Tate told Davidson of his hopes to define the rights of both scientific and theological parties. Approximating Protestant Neo-Orthodoxy's separation of scientific language and theological affirmation into separate cognitive spheres, Tate also leaned toward the fundamentalist interpretation of post-Darwinian science as "science falsely so called." He wrote:

> Science as we inherit it as Mechanism from the 17th century has nothing whatever to say about reality: if the Church or a fishmonger asserts that reality is fundamentally cheese or gold dust or Bishop Berkeley's tar water, Science has no right to deny it. On the other hand, the Church has no right to forestall *all* criticism by simply saying Science is wrong. The Church these days is of course decayed, but the attack on it should be ethical, not scientific.[106]

Though Tate never finished his proposed article, he did, however, continue to use the language of fundamentalism in his major prose works of the late 1920s: his Civil War biographies of Confederate heroes Stonewall Jackson and Jefferson Davis. Like other Agrarians, Tate cut his Agrarian teeth on the history of the War Between The States. Robert Penn Warren and Andrew Lytle, for example, also began their literary careers with non-fictional works dealing with the war. Far from promoting academic exercises in objective historical scholarship, however, the Agrarians wrote about the war in a distinctively partisan fashion. Tate used his Civil War books to engage in the culture wars then arresting the American imagination.

Warning Davidson that he would "issue a little doctrine in the book,"[107] Tate wrote *Stonewall Jackson: The Good Soldier* (1928) at the height of the fundamentalist-modernist controversy ripping apart the mainline denominations of American Protestantism. The book allowed Tate to explore in narrative form his ideas regarding the religious basis for stable culture. Contributing to what Charles Reagan Wilson has described as the first phase of the twentieth-century renewal of the South's Lost Cause civil religion,[108] he pictured the eccentric Presbyterian general as a staunch proto-fundamentalist. Fusing images of southern hagiography with the sacred rage of contemporary militant antimodernism, Tate's sympathetic portrait turned Jackson into an icon of the fierce Christian warrior. With a note of sardonic wit, Tate taunted contemporary as well as ancestral opponents. "Jackson's watchword was to deceive and mystify the enemy," he wrote. "He put his faith in God. The higher criticism of this faith is that Jackson relied upon his intellect."[109]

Tate's biography of the Confederate president Jefferson Davis rendered southern fundamentalism in even more favorable terms. Interpreting the Civil War as an East-West clash rather than a contest of North against South, Tate portrayed Confederate secessionists as the privileged carriers of beleaguered European tradition:

> Southerners believed that they stood for "Christianity and Civilization" and, seen in the light of the main traditions of Europe, the assertion was literally true: theirs was the last stand, they were the forlorn hope, of conservative Fundamentalist Christianity and of civilization, based on agrarian, class rule, in the European sense....The issue was class rule and religion *versus* democracy and science.[110]

Written in Paris, while he was on a Guggenheim Fellowship, *Jefferson Davis: His Rise and Fall* (1929) reveals the subtle influence of the expatriate experience on Tate's thought. Walter Ong has said that the "confrontation of America with Europe" perennially becomes "the problem of any serious American mind."[111] At this stage of his intellectual development, it became the central problem for Tate. Functioning prominently as a theme in the book, Europe works within a typological framework of interpretation to render the meaning of the South in a new international perspective. Narrating the attempt of Confederate diplomats to secure international recognition and assistance from Britain and France, Tate stressed the point that the failure to engage Europe sealed the fate of the South.[112] By implication, he was arguing for a view of the modern South that would link the Agrarian imperative to a larger and more durable past.

More importantly, the Jefferson Davis book reflected the author's leanings toward what Walter Lippmann was calling "the oldest fundamentalism of the western world."[113] While his antimodernist tendencies originally encouraged a rediscovery of his southern heritage, Tate ultimately turned to the literature of the European Catholic Revival to bolster his retrograde cultural criticism. Reading French authors such as Henri Bergson, Charles Péguy, Léon Bloy, and François Mauriac, and conversing with the recent convert Julian Green, he came to recognize the Catholic Church as the historic carrier of the tradition for which he longed.[114] He was also significantly influenced by writers of the English Catholic Revival, especially the historian Christopher Hollis, whose *The American Heresy* (1927) criticized the United States for promoting liberty and equality without establishing a foundational "religious authority."[115] Comparing the incipient Agrarian movement to the traditionalist Catholic movement Action Française, Tate maintained that this sort of "religious authority" was "absolutely necessary for the kind of society we want: that was the great lack of the old South."[116] In his Confederate books, he even noted how his southern subjects, Jackson and Davis, had each explored traditional Catholic teaching and, in the case of the former, considered conversion.[117]

In a *Criterion* essay solicited by the recently baptized Anglo-Catholic Eliot, Tate gathered his early Agrarian musings into a critical project that went far beyond the crisis of the American South. He stressed the necessity of "an objective religion, a universal scheme of reference" in culture.[118] Approximating Irving Babbitt's claim that "the Catholic Church may perhaps be the only institution left in the Occident that can be counted on to uphold civilized standards,"[119] Tate intimated that the Roman Catholic tradition was the vital force in Western history, the only coherent system of thought which could provide such a "scheme" and save the culture from fragmentation. Though emotionally tied to the American South, he increasingly looked to the roots of the European inheritance in search of an antidote to the ills of modernity. Informing Davidson of his personal interest in Catholicism, Tate explained its relevance to the Agrarian project: "Philosophically we must go the whole hog of reaction, and base our movement less upon the actual Old South than upon its prototype—the historical social and religious scheme of Europe. We must be the last Europeans."[120] Denouncing contemporary

Protestant liberalism as "virtually naturalism," he admitted, "I am more and more heading towards Catholicism. We have reached a condition of the spirit where no further compromise is possible."[121]

The development of Tate's negative assessment of Protestantism demonstrates why fundamentalism eventually became a problematic symbol in his antimodernist religious criticism. As Joseph Schöpp has observed, Tate's reading moved him toward an interpretation of Protestantism approximating the thesis articulated by German sociologist Max Weber in his classic, *The Protestant Ethic and the Spirit of Capitalism*.[122] For Tate, the Protestant tradition's close association with the civilization of capitalism made it a world view hardly compatible with radical Agrarian critiques of bourgeois industrialism. Furthermore, Tate's belief in the downward motion of Western history drove him to agree with Catholic social critics of the day who traced philosophical naturalism back to the intellectual ferment of the Reformation era.[123] Consequently, when Tate contributed his essay on religion to the 1930 Agrarian anthology *I'll Take My Stand*, even sympathetic readers judged it less than successful. Originally designed as a "bellicose" defense of southern fundamentalism,[124] "Remarks on the Southern Religion" declared that "the South never created a fitting religion."[125] Insinuating that Roman Catholicism would have been the appropriate faith for the feudal Old South, Tate subverted the Agrarian investment in the literary value of fundamentalism.

Still, into the early 1930s, Tate occasionally employed rural fundamentalism as a type in his critical discourse. In a 1931 open letter to the *Atlanta Journal* he wrote: "Religion in our industrial communities is practically dead. Only in the more backward, rural communities, which are communities in a real sense, and not simply economic organizations, does religion thrive."[126] Similarly, three years later, he exclaimed, "Fundamentalism, fortunately...still reigns [in the South]."[127] By that time, however, his attachment to the metaphor was mitigated by his mounting unsubstantiated assertions linking southern supernaturalism more "to Aquinas than to Calvin, Wesley, or Knox."[128]

More and more, Tate's peculiar use of fundamentalism revealed the Catholic sources of his Southern Agrarianism. In the turbulent decade after the Scopes trial, believing that modern society required the informing authority of determined belief, the young Allen Tate looked to the maligned faith of southern evangelicals as the best available example of an authoritative religion still integrally related to a coherent social order. The internal logic of his evolving Agrarian theory of religion, however, led the cautious atheist to reject the Protestant tradition as fundamentally flawed. In the early days of the crusade against industrialism and its spiritual allies, Tate manufactured a sympathy for the putative vulgarity of intractable fundamentalism, but his "fundamentalism" functioned within Agrarian discourse as a prophetic sign of contradiction. Unrestrained by fundamentalism's native critique of the Roman Catholic tradition, Tate's use of the conservative evangelical rhetoric of protest cleared the way for his endorsement of another sort of fundamentalism: Catholic antimodernism.

3 | The Cause of the Land

Trouble with your Xtianity is that it is a sham cult cut off from agriculture. Steam roller no substitute for plow.
                              —Ezra Pound to George Santayana[1]

The Scopes trial attracted worldwide attention. In Britain, G. K. Chesterton, no stranger to the controversy over evolution, keenly observed the course of the trial and recognized the urgency of the issues involved in the case. Like the Southern Agrarians, he resented "the custom to make fun of Fundamentalism and to suggest that American religion is rather antiquated." He acknowledged a grudging respect for the profound social critique buried beneath the surface of fundamentalist doctrine. Like Tate, though, Chesterton found American Protestant fundamentalism a truncated version of authentic Christianity: "Whatever else the Fundamentalist is, he is not fundamental. He is content with the bare letter of Scripture...without venturing to ask for its original authority."[2] For Chesterton, as for Tate, fundamentalism was an orphan orthodoxy—Christian truth without Christian church or Christian civilization, and this deficiency was what rendered it an unfit contributor to contemporary discussions of pressing social questions. Despite its critical instincts, it could not mount a full-scale assault on modernity, because it did not possess the necessary kind of moral authority accumulated over centuries by a tradition's transactions with the world. The Catholic sources of Tate's Agrarianism, therefore, entailed more than an emotional distaste for modernity; they grounded his Agrarian critique in an elaborate vision of society shaped by an historic tradition of social teaching.

Reconstructing the Social Order

The Catholic Revival's antimodernist spirituality that Tate encountered in the years following the Scopes trial entailed a charged critique of the economic culture dominating Western nations. Industrialism, aggravating the breakdown of the modern mind, came to represent for many Catholic observers the debilitation of the body of Western civilization, divorced from meaningful contact with the land. Fueled by the call of recent papal encyclicals for "reconstruction of the social order," Catholic critics argued for the retrieval of premodern social structures to establish a "third way" between the twin totalitarian threats of capitalism and communism. Along with secular promoters of back-to-the-land schemes and economic decentralization, some Catholic theorists advanced programs for social change based on the conviction that "Christianity was incompatible with an urbanized industrial order."[3]

Papal teaching of the era sowed the seeds for a critique of the culture of industrialism. Leo XIII's *Rerum novarum* (1891) functioned as the *Magna Charta* for the Catholic Revival's approach to social problems.[4] Mainly concerned with the rights and duties of labor and capital, the document addressed labor's right to organize, the legitimacy of collective bargaining, and the requirement of a just wage. *Rerum novarum* also articulated basic principles of social justice: the priority of the person in relation to the state, the independence of the family from governmental intrusion, and the principle of the common good. Conscious of the threat of socialism, Leo offered a forceful defense of private property: "Man not only should possess the fruits of the earth, but also the very soil." Most importantly, Leo linked social justice to a renovation of Christian culture: "If human society is to be healed now, in no other way can it be healed save by a return to Christian life and Christian institutions."[5]

Forty years later, Pius XI's *Quadragesimo anno* (1931) continued the legacy of Leo's economic teaching. Like Leo, Pius deplored the huge numbers of propertyless workers and rural wage earners and urged "the Christian renewal of all social life." More explicitly than his predecessor, he attempted to steer a middle course between free market liberalism and state-run socialism. Writing in the wake of the Russian Revolution and in the midst of the Great Depression, he addressed the dramatic developments that had changed the economic scene since Leo's time. The spirit of individualism, associated with laissez-faire capitalism, threatened to erode the rich public life that had once mediated the complex set of negotiations between individual persons and their government. By contrast, economic collectivism, the child of liberalism, inevitably led to the "moral, juridical, and social modernism," of which Pius warned in *Ubi arcano* (1922). As a guide for identifying the proper alternative to these oppressive systems, Pius proposed what became a standard piece of Catholic social teaching, the decentralist principle of subsidiarity:

> Just as it is gravely wrong to take from individuals what they can accomplish by their own initiative and industry and give it to the community, so also it is an injustice and at the same time a grave evil and disturbance of right order to assign to a greater and higher association what lesser and subordinate organizations can do.[6]

Throughout the first decades of the twentieth century, the social encyclicals of Leo and Pius inspired the participation of countless lay people in Catholic Action and instigated the establishment of numerous Catholic organizations dedicated to Christianizing the social realm. They enhanced the social consciousness that characterized the full range of modern Christian thought. The documents also became the basis for a distinctively Catholic theology of labor. Together they comprised the "Christian social manifesto" that shaped the thought of American social theorists John A. Ryan and Joseph C. Husslein, the political populism of "radio priest" Charles E. Coughlin, and the existentialist philosophy of French personalist Emmanuel Mounier.[7]

"Before There Was Any Sin"

While some Catholic social theorists applied the teachings of the papal encyclicals to plans for reforming the structures of modern industrial order, many Catholic Revival writers used the authority of the popes in their efforts to discredit industrialism entirely. Relying upon what Gene Burns has called the "ancien régime" or "neofeudal" perspective of the social encyclicals,[8] they interpreted the documents not as a call to reformation but as a summons to resistance. Proponents of the Catholic Revival denounced modern commerce as essentially anti-Christian. As an alternative, they proposed a strategic return to a pattern of agricultural simplicity in fundamental conflict with the prevailing spirit of modernity. Some even advocated physical withdrawal from the "dark, satanic mills" of the West's industrialized cities.

In England, popular Catholic apologists G. K. Chesterton and Hilaire Belloc became the Revival's most vocal critics of the commercial civilization spawned by industrialism. Derided by their opponents with the unflattering nickname of "Chesterbelloc," the two writers invested their social criticism with verbal sallies against the imperatives of industrial economy. They attacked all aspects of the societal infrastructure that fostered a regimented culture of consumerism: modern

advertising, compulsory universal education, bureaucratic government, political paternalism, and mass transportation. In contrast to
Catholic social critics who emphasized the primary category of justice,
Chesterton and Belloc argued their case on the basis of liberty. For
them, the modern economic order boiled down to one thing: the
shrinking margin of individual freedom. Their libertarian politics led
them to espouse a Catholic agrarianism which placed liberty and property in close moral alignment.[9]

Belloc articulated this position in *The Servile State* (1912) and *The
Restoration of Property* (1936). Western history, according to Belloc, illus-
trated how the rise and fall of the free individual was linked to
the growth and decay of European Catholic culture. He organized the
history of this relationship into three stages. First, the triumph of classical
Christian culture liberated much of Europe's population from the economic servitude of pagan society. Next, medieval Christendom became
the patron of a free and just order, a "distributist" or "proprietary" society committed to "the establishment of a State in which men should be
economically free through the possession of capital and land." Finally,
the collapse of Christendom, hastened by the modern commercial revo-
lutions of free enterprise and collectivism, represented the West's tragic
slip back into a state of political and economic subjection. In the twentieth-century condition of advanced industrialism, both capitalism and
socialism represented outdated options, dwarfed by the emerging giant
of the state-regulated economy. "The future of industrial society," he
said, "is a future in which subsistence and security shall be guaranteed for
the Proletariat, but shall be guaranteed at the expense of the old political
freedom and by the establishment of that Proletariat in a status really,
though not nominally, servile."[10]

It was no accident that Belloc identified England and Germany as
the locations where capitalism had evolved into what he called the post-
capitalist "servile state." He blamed Protestantism's social alliance with
the mercantile class for the destruction of the medieval guilds, the
demise of a free peasantry, and the rise of the plutocratic state. He
especially focused on the sixteenth-century seizure of Catholic Church
property and its allotment to supporters of the burgeoning English
nation-state as twin harbingers of a new economic system barring the
mass of citizens from ownership and thereby the basis of true freedom.
Composed of "wage slaves," forced into exchanging their freedom for
the economic security of the centralized welfare state, the modern
"servile state," in Belloc's opinion, depended upon a distinctly anti-
Catholic philosophy of social organization. Only in rural France and
Ireland, where elements of folk Catholicism survived, did he discover

remnants of the "distributist state" of the Middle Ages. "We must convert England to a right religion," he declared, "before we can make Englishmen free."[11]

Chesterton, too, saw few signs of hope in an economic order where the individual land owner was rapidly becoming an endangered species. Like Belloc, he initially thought Old World peasants virtually the last representatives of the West's once dominant agrarian culture. After his visit to the United States, however, Chesterton expressed admiration for the not-so-Catholic culture of the American South. "Old England," he said, "might still be traced in Old Dixie."[12] Staking his career on the value of common sense and the virtue of the common person, Chesterton turned his well-honed gift of satire on the uncommon madness of modern economics. In *The Outline of Sanity* (1926), he found big business and big government jointly culpable for the oppressive mechanization and drab mediocrity of the modern labor state. Educated in schools held hostage to the interests of organized commercialism, the modern individual, he asserted, entered the work force stripped of creativity, enamored of luxury, and oblivious to the "grinding slavery of his leisure." Even more disturbing, he claimed, was the modern person's addictive dependence upon the moralism of the state, which dictated acceptable levels of health, intelligence, and income. To Chesterton, the modern bureaucratic economy ran according to a politically sanctioned ideology that "utterly distrusts a man."[13] Like Belloc, Chesterton favored the model of medieval agrarian society, because he sought an order of community that recognized the dignity of labor and the moral responsibility of the individual. He even found himself in the awkward position of defending the right to be poor and ignorant without state interference. Agrarian economics and Christian humanism, he thought, best served the human condition.[14]

Together, Belloc and Chesterton provided the intellectual leadership for the Catholic Land movement in Britain. A loose coalition of individuals and groups advocating everything from political anarchism to the preservation of folk culture, the movement captured the spirit of Catholic discontent with modern society. In general, the movement linked the future of European culture to a recovery of man's natural and historic relationship to the land. Specifically, it endorsed a Catholic agrarian philosophy dubbed "Distributism," after Belloc's description of the virtues of medieval economics. Fueled by the social criticism published by "Chesterbelloc" in *New Witness* and *G. K.'s Weekly*, the movement's activities led to the founding of the Distributist League in 1926.

As defined by members of the League, Distributism sought to express fidelity to the values emphasized in the social encyclicals of the modern popes: private property, workers' rights, and subsidiarity. Beyond that, it supported a return to premodern institutions associated with an agriculturally based economy. According to Jay P. Corrin, the movement's ideal was "a balanced or mixed economy of independent farmers and small industries owned and operated by the workers themselves."[15] Sources of inspiration included earlier witnesses against modernity, such as the eighteenth-century country life advocate William Cobbett, the artists of the Pre-Raphaelite Brotherhood, and other Victorian critics of modern Europe, like William Morris and John Ruskin. Some Distributists also traced lines of spiritual ancestry back to the machine-smashing Luddites of early-nineteenth-century England.

Britain's Catholic Distributists involved themselves in a variety of activities. While some dreamed of a neo-feudalist utopia, others plotted boycotts of chain stores and omnibus companies. Still others sought to remedy the ugliness of modern civilization with a revival of traditional handicrafts and ancient church architecture. Some, like Chesterton, were mainly "paper agrarians." Their ideas filled the pages of Catholic periodicals such as *The Cross and the Plough*, applying Distributism to an array of issues from monopolies and taxation to birth control and divorce, but they conducted their campaign against the culture of industrialism from their urban offices and townhouses. Other Distributists, obeying the logic of their critique, literally did "flee to the fields."[16] They became the Catholic parallels to the Zionist pioneers establishing *kibbutzim* in the land of Palestine.

Belloc, for example, settled his family in King's Land, a rustic house on five acres in the middle of what his biographer calls "a benign and not a hostile nowhere."[17] Eric Gill, the multi-talented artist, writer, and Dominican tertiary, co-founded a self-sufficient Distributist collective village at Ditchling in Sussex, where members dedicated their days to agriculture, craftsmanship, and communal prayer.[18] Even publishers Frank Sheed and Maisie Ward, whose company put many Distributist works into print, experimented with agrarian living.[19] Few Distributists, however, embodied their convictions the way Vincent McNabb did. Traveling everywhere on foot and in a habit of homespun, the outspoken Dominican priest became a stark symbol of Distributist primitivism. Famous for his outdoor preaching and his refusal to use modern conveniences, McNabb infused the movement with a spirituality based on asceticism and voluntary poverty.[20] In all its eccentricity and idealism, the agrarian tradition of the Catholic Revival achieved its summation in Pope Pius XII's declaration: "Before there was any sin, God gave man the earth for his cultivation as the most beautiful and honorable occupation in the natural order."[21]

"The Chosen People of God"

Like their British counterparts, American proponents of the Catholic Revival also drew agrarian conclusions from the new ventures in Catholic social teaching. They formed organizations, supported periodicals, and proposed programs that stressed "the enduring values of local identity and community, the importance of family stability, love of the land, the celebration of yearly rituals, and local cultural tradition."[22] Shaped by the particulars of their own history and the unique landscape of their continent, Catholic agrarians in the United States gave their efforts a distinctively American character.

By the early twentieth century, agrarianism had long been a feature of the American intellectual tradition.[23] A subspecies of what Peter J. Schmitt has called the back-to-nature arcadian myth in America,[24] it shared the belief that human well-being depends upon meaningful contact with nature, but invested the middle landscape of cultivated ground with particular political and moral value. According to Edward S. Shapiro, the agrarian myth augmented America's love of nature with the conviction

> that only in a society dominated by farms and small towns [can] individualism, independence, cultural stability, the widespread ownership of property, economic freedom, political and social conservatism, a strong family life, and religion flourish.[25]

The phases of American agrarianism since the colonial period correspond roughly to the changing paradigms governing the evolution of the nation's economic organization. In the commercial culture of the eighteenth century, for example, agrarianism assumed the role of a noble social ideal. Fearing the consequences of an industrialized United States independent of the rule of nature, Thomas Jefferson hoped to freeze the Enlightenment's bourgeois revolution in its early stage. He envisioned a mixture of home and craft industry as the best economic structure to revive ancient virtue and protect New World liberty. Securing a place for republican husbandry in the American hierarchy of values, he praised tillers of the soil as "the chosen people of God," thereby inaugurating what Jan Wojcik has called a "wisdom literature of farming" in U.S. cultural life.[26]

As the work ethic of revolutionary yeomen gave way to the production ethic of industrial workers, agrarianism became a mode of political revolt in the next century. Even while Emerson praised the vocation of the common American farmer and Thoreau played the romantic agriculturalist in his bean field, farmer unrest began to disturb the garden of antebellum America. Especially in the expanding credit economy of the post–Civil War nation, radical agrarian democracy developed as the protest movement of a new rural underclass. Agrarian activists mounted fierce opposition to unregulated transportation trusts, national banks, produce and stock exchanges, the gold standard, and the tariff—all the elements contributing to a post-agrarian American economy. Often the movement sparked violent outbursts. Growing out of the Granger movement and the Farmer Alliances of southern and midwestern states, the Populist movement attempted to enlist American farmers into a mass political party.[27]

After Populism's defeat in the presidential election of 1896, radical agrarianism exerted minimal influence in American society. In the consumer culture of modernist society, twentieth-century agrarianism functioned as a call for spiritual renewal. As the moralized economy of Victorian production gave rise to the psychologized economy of modern acquisitiveness, the American subsistence farmer rushed toward extinction. Once the dominant group in American society, by 1920 the farm population had plummeted to just 30 percent of the population. In response to the demise of American farming, a new agrarian myth surfaced. Viewing the crisis as moral and not simply economic, advocates of "higher agrarianism" turned the myth into a mode of social prophecy.[28]

The Country Life movement at the turn of the century sparked renewed interest in the American agrarian tradition.[29] Though scores of writers proposed plans to repatriate urbanites on the land, much of the twentieth-century's "romantic agrarianism" was polemical in character rather than directed toward practical projects for change. Agrarianism offered a rhetorical vehicle for a new wave of anti-urban sentiment in the nation.[30] Periodicals like Gustav Stickley's *Craftsman* and Bernarr MacFadden's *Liberty* magazine placed this feeling in the context of a wide-ranging form of antimodernist discourse. They explained the phenomenon of modern America as a mass rejection of quality in goods, beauty in art, responsibility in government, and pride in workmanship. Those themes played a prominent role in Ralph Borsodi's *This Ugly Civilization* (1929), a Nietzschean critique of modern society's aesthetic poverty and the human "automatons" afraid to challenge it.[31] In a different fashion, Liberty Hyde Bailey, Cornell University's "philosopher of country life," focused his agrarianism on the spiritual consequences of industrialism. Concerned that "earth righteousness" was vanishing just as rapidly as rural America, he believed farm living the way to replenish the moral imagination eroded by the frenzied materialism of urban life.[32]

"The Spiritual Riches of Farm Living"

Secular theorists, of course, were not the only Americans concerned about the nation's transformation into an urban and spiritual wasteland. Contributing to a parallel Country Life movement in the churches, Protestant leaders drew upon the resources of their traditions in order to halt the erosion of the rural culture enshrined in American myth and history.[33] Church-related colleges, with roots in the manual labor movement of the nineteenth century, reminded many young Americans of the link between virtuous character and the agrarian tradition. In addition, Protestant denominations formed new agencies intentionally created to address the problems of farmers and promote the ideals of rural living. By the 1920s, most Protestant bodies had developed Rural Life ministries commissioned to attend to the needs of farm families. Mainline organizations, such as the Church and Country Life Department of the Presbyterian Church U.S.A., relied upon the new disciplines of sociology and social work to bolster their pastoral efforts. Imitating President Theodore Roosevelt's Country Life Association, they functioned virtually as a wing of the progressive movement.[34] Other groups, such as the Southern Baptist Home Mission Board, funded rural ventures in order to help farmer-preachers stem the tide of modernism in small-town America.[35] Even the Social Gospel movement, usually associated with attempts to reform industrial society, worked to save the American farm. While the foremost Social Gospel advocate, northern Baptist theologian Walter Rauschenbusch, maintained that "the mass of independent farmers have been and still are the moral backbone of our nation,"[36] some ministers began preaching a full-fledged "agricultural Social Gospel."[37]

Within the U.S. Catholic community, agrarian thought also enjoyed a time-honored position of respect. Nineteenth-century immigration patterns established American Catholicism predominantly as an urban religion, but, as Jay Dolan has demonstrated, even members of New York City's immigrant church embraced the national ideal of the moral superiority of pastoral and rural life.[38] From the founding of Maryland to the early twentieth century, private colonization efforts and federal settlement programs lured Catholics from eastern cities to the nation's interior. Irish-born Catholics joined the ranks of plantation gentry in the Old South and purchased rich land in the upper Midwest. Similarly, German and Scandinavian Catholics followed the path of westward expansion, building agricultural colonies in the prairie states. As Martin Schirber has observed, "the relationship between Catholics and the American farm is a significant part of the experience of the Church in this country."[39]

In the early twentieth century, the agrarian tradition of Catholicism flourished in the atmosphere of nationwide discontent with urbanization and industrialization. During this period, Catholics made significant contributions to the American agrarian tradition. The British Distributist movement, for example, attracted a number of non-Catholic intellectuals disenchanted with the trends of modern society. Advertising executive Ralph Borsodi, social critic Lewis Mumford, architect Frank Lloyd Wright, agriculture expert O. E. Baker, and journalist Herbert Agar were among the American elites who drew inspiration from the English Catholic Land movement. At the same time, American agrarian impulses gained momentum from themes in the larger Catholic Revival. Catholic antimodernism, romantic medievalism, papal emphasis on the Mystical Body of Christ, and the quest for a new Christendom led many religious and secular critics to re-examine the agrarian heritage of Catholicism and to elevate life on the land as the perfect context for meaningful faith and human community.

After 1900, as American Catholicism increasingly developed a nationwide denominational structure, the U.S. Catholic Church gave ecclesiastical form to its agrarian concerns, creating what eventually became a genuine Catholic Rural Life movement in America.[40] Founded in 1920 by Minnesota native Father Edwin O'Hara, the Catholic Rural Life Bureau, the agrarian wing of the National Catholic Welfare Council (later, Conference), endeavored to enhance the dignity of farming as a Christian vocation and strengthen the Catholic presence in rural America.[41] Following O'Hara's lead, American Catholics threw themselves into rural work. The decades after the First World War witnessed a proliferation of Catholic agrarian literature and special interest groups. Emerging as the umbrella organization in 1922, the National Catholic Rural Life Conference (NCRLC) cast a sacred canopy over a thriving network of agrarian movements and experiments. *Rural Notes*, *St. Isidore's Plow*, *Catholic Rural Life*, and *Landward* kept agrarian ideas before the public, while the NCRLC's *Manifesto on Rural Life* (1939) presented a systematic policy toward agriculture "chiefly derived from Catholic social philosophy."[42] Especially active in the Depression years, the NCRLC channeled its resources into an aggressive crusade to save rural America.[43] Its first president, Father Howard Bishop, founded the Glenmary missioners to evangelize what he called America's "No Priest Land," and his successor, Monsignor Luigi Ligutti, gained fame as a tireless advocate of rural church life.[44] The Conference even won Pius XII's blessing for a campaign promoting devotion to St. Isidore, the twelfth-century Spanish peasant canonized as the patron of farmers.[45]

Catholic religious orders in America also responded with vigor to the agrarian gospel. For example, the Benedictine monks of Minnesota made St. John's Abbey a national center for rural life education. Integrating his philosophy of rural life into a total vision of Catholic faith and identity, Benedictine priest Virgil Michel conceived of Catholic agrarianism as a unitive force embracing social justice, intellectual growth, and liturgical renewal.[46] In addition, midwestern Jesuits ordained St. Mary's College in Kansas the headquarters for the agrarian pursuits of their Society. There, seminarians published tracts on rural sociology and conducted experiments in "biodynamic agriculture."[47] As Peter McDonough has observed in his study of the twentieth-century Jesuit community, American members of the order found in their Society an intellectual atmosphere hospitable toward agrarian utopianism.[48]

Catholic agrarianism soon became a staple of the lay Catholic Revival. Church leaders commended it as a significant dimension of the laity's apostolate in the world. *Commonweal* and *Catholic Action* ran articles on agrarian themes for lay readers, and many lay people participated in NCRLC-sponsored events. The more daring attempted to put their agrarian theories into practice. Eugene and Abigail McCarthy, for instance, sought to experience "the spiritual riches of farm living" in rural Minnesota before moving into the spotlight of national politics. For them, their St. Anne's Farm provided the context for a common life "based on the Benedictine ideal of mixed prayer and work."[49] With similar motives, Ed and Dorothy Willock, associated with *Integrity* magazine, made Marycrest farm in New York a haven for lay couples with a monastic bent.[50]

By far, the most radical form of Catholic agrarianism issued from the Catholic Worker movement originating in New York City. Organized in 1933, with the appearance of the *Catholic Worker* newspaper, the movement is best known for its inner-city houses of hospitality designed to minister to the urban poor, unemployed, and homeless. Its founders, lay activists Peter Maurin and Dorothy Day, based its mission on the church's social encyclicals, supplemented by a literal interpretation of the traditional corporal works of mercy. Opposed to the emerging American welfare and security state, they made the evangelical counsels of voluntary poverty and pacifism centerpieces of the movement's distinctive approach to social problems.[51]

Despite its reputation as a novel Catholic mission to the nation's cities, the Catholic Worker movement shared agrarian tendencies similar to those driving the Rural Life movement. As Belden Lane has noted, Maurin was essentially "a medievalist, calling for a romantic

Catholic agrarianism." The French-born theoretician of the movement, Maurin sought to renew society through a synthesis of "Cult, Culture, and Cultivation."[52] He insisted that a social strategy for secular America required the creation of farming communes where an integrated, wholesome life would be possible. In his poetic "Easy Essays," he stated the point emphatically: "The future of the Church / is on the land."[53] By the late 1930s, Catholic Worker volunteers attempted to arrest the dehumanizing drive of modern industry with the agricultural personalism of Maurin's "Green Revolution." Beginning with a tiny garden on Staten Island and twenty-eight-acre Maryfarm near Easton, Pennsylvania, the Catholic Workers, according to Day's frank analysis, "blundered our way into farming."[54]

Often identified with the New Catholic Left, the Catholic Worker movement of the pre-Vatican II era defied conventional categories of classification. Day skillfully merged sympathy for aspects of the Marxist critique with firm devotion to traditional Catholic teaching. By contrast, Ammon Hennacy, a leader within the movement during the 1950s, downplayed Catholicism, emphasizing instead the movement's kinship with radical traditions of pacifism, anarchism, and civil disobedience. For his part, Maurin expressed only disdain for the political left. He grounded the movement in the prophetic dimensions of Catholic antimodernism, medievalism, anticommunism, papal authority, and neoscholastic thought.[55] As Anthony Novitsky has suggested, Maurin's vision derived from the reactionary social thought of the European Catholic Revival.[56] In fact, Maurin identified himself as a "Radical of the Right."[57]

Edward Shapiro, a historian of decentralist movements in America between the world wars, has accurately identified an "agrarian fundamentalism" at the heart of Catholic enthusiasm for rural culture.[58] Catholic agrarians feared the loss of social tradition as much as the abuses of capitalism and communism. For them, the "third way" suggested by the encyclicals of Leo XIII and Pius XI implied a reclamation of an order of public life dominated by conservative religious values. The problem with American society, they thought, was not its traditional repression of revolutionary instincts, but its wholesale departure from tradition. Like the English Distributists, Maurin and other Catholic agrarians in America linked their love for the land to a desire for a revitalized Christian culture.

"A Feudal Society Without a Feudal Religion"

By the time he returned to America in 1930, Allen Tate was already becoming acquainted with the international currents of "agrarian fundamentalism." Since 1927, he had been corresponding with the former Fugitives on the subject of a symposium to defend the South's "agrarian way of life." During that period, Tate's antimodernism drew him increasingly into the orbit of agrarian intellectuals beyond the circle of the southern critics. His early reviews and articles appeared in the *New Republic* and *Criterion*, journals sympathetic to agrarian sentiments, and his private reading introduced him to the deep dissatisfaction with modernity expressed in the European Catholic experience. Impressed by the way Distributist historians linked Catholic social teaching to a justification of the Old South, Tate, though still an unbeliever, brought a uniquely Catholic approach to the "utopian conservatism" of what would become the Southern Agrarian movement.[59] If he went to Europe as something of a neo-Confederate, he left the expatriate literary community with an agrarian philosophy shaped by more than a reawakened sectional consciousness.

The text of Tate's first Southern Agrarian article revealed the distance between him and his colleagues. "Remarks on the Southern Religion," his essay in *I'll Take My Stand* (1930), though supposed to be an apology for southern institutions, departed from the program of the movement by wedding Southern Agrarian concerns to Catholic Revival principles. In it Tate suggested that the culture of the Old South failed because "it could not create its appropriate religion." Drawing Chestertonian parallels between the South and the traditional peasant societies of Catholic Europe, Tate stopped short of concluding that Catholicism, rather than evangelical revivalism or Jeffersonian naturalism, would have been the proper faith for the region. Like Glenmary founder Howard Bishop, he seemed to believe that the South could have been fertile ground for the Catholic faith. To him, the Old South "was a feudal society without a feudal religion," and the New South, by implication, was bereft of a spiritual legacy.[60]

Even before composing the essay, Tate showed signs of discomfort with the narrowness of the intended Southern Agrarian agenda. Initially, while deliberating the question of who should write the volume's essay on religion, Tate proposed changing the topic from Donald Davidson's straightforward "Protestantism in the South" to the more provocative subject "Religion and Aristocracy in the South." The essay, Tate thought, should address the question: "Was Southern religion in accord with social and political tendencies?"[61] Perplexed regarding the possibility of finding a suitable author for such an essay, Davidson supposed that "at a pinch" either Tate or Ransom could tackle the issue.[62] Late in 1929, before accepting the job himself, Tate recommended that the assignment go to a young Rhodes Scholar named Dixon Wecter. A fellow southerner in cultural exile, Wecter had entered the Roman Catholic Church at England's Downside Abbey just months before Tate tried to recruit him for the Agrarian cause. As Tate assured Davidson, Wecter was "a Catholic, but also a philosopher, with a philosophic view of religion very much resembling our view."[63] Pleased with Christopher Hollis' Distributist performance in *The American Heresy*,[64] Tate wanted to see how a Catholic imagination could supplement the exclusively Protestant minds running the Southern Agrarian project.

A second problem arose after the Tates and their five-year-old daughter Nancy returned to the American South. At Benfolly, their antebellum farm house near Clarksville, Tennessee, Tate drafted frantic letters voicing his objections to the limitations of the book's proposed title. *I'll Take My Stand*, taken from the popular minstrel song "Dixie," he complained, misrepresented the symposium's potentially broad purpose of cultural criticism. Not only was it an unforgivable "breach of decorum," but it risked alienating "foreign" readers blind to the complex nuances in the colloquial phrase. With his eye on the international scene, Tate argued for the alternative title *Tracts Against Communism*.[65] Suggesting a weird cross between Newman's Tractarian critique of nineteenth-century liberalism and Belloc's Distributist rejection of the modern "servile state," Tate's awkward title betrayed the Catholic trajectory of his evolving Agrarian thought. Despite the Confederate memorabilia adorning his rustic Benfolly, Tate's Agrarianism increasingly exhibited an undeniably catholic (and Catholic) quality.

Nearly derailing the publication process of *I'll Take My Stand*, Tate's resistance to the restricted focus of the symposium drove an ideological wedge between him and the other contributors. In the end, he agreed to write the book's essay on religion himself, but he felt obliged to print a disclaimer differentiating his Agrarianism from that of his colleagues. As a footnote to "Remarks on the Southern Religion," he wrote:

> The writer is constrained to point out...that in his opinion the general title of this book is not quite true to its aims. It emphasizes the fact of exclusiveness rather than its benefits; it points to a particular house but omits to say that it was the home of a spirit that may also have lived elsewhere....[66]

In his history of *The Southern Agrarians*, Paul Conkin has attempted to explain Tate's curious ambivalence, maintaining that Tate "wanted to emphasize, not the historical South, but certain religious values that found lodgement in that South."[67] Though this thesis gives due credit to the letter of Tate's words, a critical reading of the essay discloses evidence inviting another conclusion. In fact, Tate's contribution to *I'll Take My Stand* takes pains to assert that the South never fully possessed the "spirit" of authentic agrarian culture. When he examined the temple of his region's past, he discovered to his dismay that the ark was actually empty. Though the South never submitted to the "heresy" of New England, he said, its naturally religious instinct remained "inchoate and unorganized." According to Tate,

> The South would not have been defeated had it possessed a suffi-
> cient faith in its own kind of God. It would not have been defeated,
> in other words, had it been able to bring out a body of doctrine set-
> ting forth its true conviction that the ends of man require more for
> their realization than politics.[68]

With no *summa* of theological and moral imagination at hand—no racial tradition of native fantasy or epic drama—America's southerners never possessed the resources required to articulate the mythic vision necessary for a successful agrarian culture. Southerners, he lamented, "have been inferior to the Irish in this virtue."[69]

"Radicals of the Right"

Published in the autumn of 1930, *I'll Take My Stand* remains the most significant piece of literature in the Southern Agrarian canon. For the "Twelve Southerners" involved in its making, however, it was only the beginning of a movement that dominated their lives through much of the following decade. The chief members of the symposium postponed, and in some cases risked, the advancement of academic and literary careers, expending much energy and scarce financial resources on lec-tures, publications, and meetings devoted to the Agrarian effort. Aside from the mixed blessing of linking his name permanently to unpopular southern causes, Tate's role in the movement set the stage for collabora-tive involvement with representatives of the Catholic Revival.

First, Tate's mentors increased his exposure to Catholic Revival ideas and personalities relevant to his Agrarianism, reaffirming his broad con-ception of the movement and his fledgling commitment to Catholic social thought. In the early 1930s, for example, John Crowe Ransom and T. S. Eliot expressed interest in the agrarian social criticism enlivening the English Catholic community. Both men endeavored to draw paral-lels between it and the work of the Southern Agrarians. Ransom, who despite his bias against Catholicism had been impressed with Chesterton on his 1921 American tour, established a vital link between the Southern

Agrarian community and the Catholic historian Christopher Dawson. From 1931 to 1932, while studying economics in England on a Guggenheim Fellowship, Ransom befriended the famous convert, tapping his intelligence for resources that might contribute to his proposed book on agrarian economics. To Tate he wrote, "Chris Dawson knows more religion and philosophy and economics than any young man I have ever met."[70] Similarly, Eliot publicly went on record in favor of Catholic Distributism, seasoning his urbane literary criticism with ravaging reviews of modern industrialism. In his 1933 Page-Barbour Lectures at the University of Virginia, later published as *After Strange Gods*, he made an explicit connection between his defense of "traditional wisdom" and the work of the Distributists and the Agrarians. Posing as a "Yankee" familiar with the horrors of a culture divorced from agriculture, Eliot endorsed "Mr. Allen Tate and his friends," while also acknowledging his intellectual debts to "Mr. Chesterton and his 'distributism,' Mr. Christopher Dawson...and Mr. [Maurice] Reckitt," the Christian Socialist leader on the board of *G. K.'s Weekly*.[71]

Secondly, Tate's own writing increased his contacts with the agrarians of the Catholic Revival and enlarged his theory of Agrarianism. From 1933 to 1937, while struggling to sustain a literary vocation with temporary teaching assignments, Tate contributed regularly to a newly founded periodical called the *American Review*. Designed by its neoconservative editor Seward Collins as the successor to his neo-Humanist *Bookman*, the new journal functioned as a vehicle for the cultural discontent of "Radicals of the Right."[72] In the journal, dismissed by historian Samuel Eliot Morison as "the organ of an American fascist party,"[73] Tate's essays on unemployment, the ideal of the traditional society, and other subjects appeared next to articles by well-known writers of the international Catholic Revival.[74] The journal showcased the works of the principal Distributist writers, Chesterton, Belloc, and Gill, while introducing American readers to other Distributists such as Vincent McNabb, Harold Robbins, Hilary Pepler, Douglas Jerrold, John C. Rawe, and anti-machinery extremist Arthur J. Penty.[75] The journal also opened its pages to respected Revival writers such as Eliot, Dawson, the English Jesuit Martin D'Arcy, and the Russian émigré philosopher Nicholas Berdyaev. Though not technically Distributists, these critics promoted a strain of Christian social thought consistent with the journal's agrarian emphases. According to the editor, one of the chief purposes of the magazine was "to make better known the economic views of the English group who call themselves Distributists."[76]

Editor Collins was at least partially responsible for reinforcing Tate's inclination toward Distributist social theory. Boasting of his journal's popularity among subscribers in Catholic convents and seminaries, he wrote to Tate expressing his "delight that you found so much congenial in the Belloc-Chesterton books."[77] From that time on, although he never developed much of a taste for Chesterton's light-footed sense of paradox, Tate laced his criticism with deferential references to the more sober Belloc. In fact, *The Servile State* became something of a prophetic text for him.[78] Writing to John Peale Bishop in 1933, he revealed his affinity for the English Catholic agrarians:

> I was astonished to learn that the Distributists, with some minor differences of terms, have precisely our point of view, which of course is briefly: the dole must be capitalized and its beneficiaries instead of remaining idle must be returned to the land. The big basic industries must be broken up and socialized, and the small businesses returned to the people. The Distributists differ with us on this in no respect. The end in view is the destruction of the middle class-capitalist hegemony, and the restoration with the material at hand, not a literal restoration, of traditional society.[79]

A third factor responsible for integrating Tate into the Catholic agrarian network was his association with southern journalist and historian Herbert Agar. After earning a Ph.D. at Princeton, Agar became acquainted with Distributist thought while serving as London correspondent for the Louisville *Courier-Journal* newspaper. He came to the attention of Tate as author of *The People's Choice* (1933), the Pulitzer Prize–winning history of the American Presidency. In Agar, Tate found someone in tune with the Agrarian protest against mass culture as well as his desire to combine forces with Catholics agitating for similar goals. Though never a practicing member of the Roman Catholic Church, Agar's sympathy toward Catholicism earned him the respect of leaders in the Catholic Rural Life movement.[80]

Together, Tate and Agar planned a joint Agrarian-Distributist symposium. As early as 1933, Tate contacted Agar, mentioning the idea of a second Agrarian anthology. Hoping to enlist Eliot and Dawson, in addition to the original Southern Agrarians, Tate explained his rationale for such a project:

> We have, I think, only one dogma, against the pseudo-metaphysical dogma of capitalist-communist philosophy: that men can still make the kind of society morally that they want, and that machine-technology has not changed the political nature of men.[81]

Everything, he said, is based upon one firm conviction: "agrarianism is not dead. It is an old instinct waiting for its political philosophy to be restored."[82]

In a draft of a letter to the publishing house Harper and Brothers, Tate defined the objectives of the book in terms of a "general Conservative Revolution" against the "heresy" of industrial capitalism.[83] A month later, he sent a revised letter to the same firm, describing how the work would address the "universal implications" of the Agrarianism incompletely handled in *I'll Take My Stand*. Listing twelve potential chapters, he included sketches of an article on religion and economics by Eliot, a discussion of "romantic mediaevalism" in English agrarianism by Agrarian veteran Robert Penn Warren, a treatment of the "Dehumanization of economics" by Agar, and a critique of the "superstition of Technological Determinism" to be written by himself.[84]

Finally appearing in 1936, *Who Owns America? A New Declaration of Independence* represented a coalition of anti-industrialist Catholics, Protestants, and other "third-way" critics of the modern social order. A collection of Depression-era essays edited by Agar and Tate, the book argued that

> monopoly capitalism is evil and self-destructive, and that it is possible, while preserving private ownership, to build a true democracy in which men would be better off both morally and physically, more likely to attain that inner peace which is the mark of a good life.[85]

More importantly, it documented Tate's place in the emerging Agrarian-Distributist community. The roster of writers who eventually contributed to the book, though still dominated by Southern Agrarian stalwarts, included key individuals from the world of Catholic social criticism. Douglas Jerrold, outspoken apologist for Franco and Mussolini in the *English Review*, wrote on the future of European society; Belloc, by then in his sixties, provided the book's Distributist *imprimatur* in a chapter on "The Modern Man"; American Jesuit John C. Rawe delivered the perspective of the Catholic rural movement in "Agriculture and the Property State."[86] Though Agar privately despaired of ever "putting Rawe's piece into something resembling English,"[87] Rawe's involvement in the project revealed how well the editors had succeeded in incorporating the U.S. Catholic agrarian mainstream into their work. Uncharitably dubbed the "Edgar Guest of regional planning" by a contemporary historian of the Jesuits,[88] Rawe, associated with Saint Louis University and St. Mary's College, became a leading figure in American Catholic agrarianism with the publication of his articles in the *Modern Schoolman* and his 1940 text, *Rural Roads to Security* (co-written with Monsignor Luigi Ligutti).[89]

Favorably received in the Catholic press,[90] *Who Owns America?* testified to only one part of the Tate-Agar partnership. While editing the anthology, Tate was also instrumental in organizing a national Alliance of Agrarian and Distributist Groups, a network of non-Marxist critics of capitalism designed to perpetuate the cooperative spirit begun by collaboration on the book. More politically astute than Tate, Agar thought the Catholic Land movement would be an important partner in such a venture. His letters kept Tate abreast of current developments within the movement, including enthusiastic reports regarding cooperatives among Catholic farmers and fishermen in Nova Scotia.[91] Nevertheless, Agar warned against alienating Protestants engaged in similar work. Earlier, he had intentionally invited Cleanth Brooks to contribute an essay to *Who Owns America?* in order to provide Protestant balance to Belloc's strongly Catholic article. The son of a Methodist pastor and a recent addition to the Southern Agrarians, Brooks had already established for himself a track record as a Protestant critic of modernism in the *American Review*. Now, Agar was concerned lest the movement be known as simply a Catholic phenomenon.[92]

As it turned out, his fears had some basis in reality. At its first meeting, the organization of Agrarians and Distributists counted among its most active members Father Rawe and fellow Jesuit priests Edward Day Stewart from Saint Louis University and Charles C. Chapman from Loyola University in New Orleans.[93] Some participants even hoped to meet jointly with the National Catholic Rural Life Conference at its upcoming convention on the campus of Saint Louis University,[94] but many of the plans for collaboration never materialized. According to Paul Conkin, internal conflicts plagued the Alliance during its brief existence.[95] It did, however, give additional exposure to the concerns of Agrarianism nationwide, just as it furthered Tate's entrance into Catholic intellectual circles. Despite its failings, the Alliance led to plans for events such as a Northwestern University conference on social justice, to which Tate was invited along with Catholic heavyweights Virgil Michel, John A. Ryan, and Hilaire Belloc.[96]

At the same time, Tate and Agar corresponded regarding the establishment of a journal to keep Agrarian-Distributist ideas before the public. Wary of further association with the openly fascist Seward Collins, Tate sought to free himself from the *American Review* and charges of uncritical medievalism.[97] He still hoped to find a journal hospitable to all forms of agrarianism. Likewise, the Agrarian-

Distributist Alliance itself eagerly pursued the idea of an independent magazine, seeking Tate's leadership in the matter. Some of the original Agrarians, when faced with the proposal, feared the loss of their movement's integrity. Tate understood the misgivings of his Nashville brethren but had no objections to the journal providing a forum for agrarians of all stripes. "There is no reason," he said, "why the Catholics, the cooperatives, the Homesteaders, [and] the single-taxers cannot all be represented in our pages."[98]

When the journal, *Free America*, finally became a reality, Tate faithfully supported it, even serving as an editor during the lean period of 1939–1940. By then, however, the Southern Agrarian movement had passed its unitive and productive phase. The southern "symposium," never truly a harmonious project from the start, began to show how much it had suffered from a decade of disagreements among its membership over basic policy and philosophy. "The whole agrarian movement," Tate confessed late in 1935, "has become a reproach."[99] Tate ended his active career as an Agrarian publicist at the close of the decade, having, as one observer put it, "larger philosophical goals to pursue."[100]

Despite these developments, the original vision of the restoration of traditional agrarian society never fully departed from Tate's philosophy of humane culture. To a significant degree, the "larger philosophical goals" of his later career were initially fostered by his appropriation of Catholic Revival social thought. At the conclusion of his Southern Agrarian work, Tate's relationship with the agrarian critics of the Catholic Revival had been firmly established. One thing was certain: if Tate's criticism of modern society were to continue, it would carry the imprint of his intimacy with Catholic agrarianism.

In "A Personal Statement on Fascism," written to dissociate himself from "all forms of totalitarianism," Tate made it clear how far he identified with the Catholic critique of modern society:

> I am not and have never been a political writer; but in so far as my interests as a literary critic have made it necessary for me to examine the social implications of literature, I have written essays which set forth the desirability, as the best basis for democratic independence, of what has been called the "distributist" or agrarian society.[101]

Those critics who in the early 1930s had suspected him of harboring friendly, if vague, sympathies toward "popery" betrayed a greater degree of perception than Tate wished to admit.[102] By 1940, when

Christopher Dawson invited him to write for the English Catholic quarterly, *New Dublin Review*, Tate was already well versed in the main doctrines of Catholicism's hope to restructure the social order.[103]

"A Fanatical Devotion"

Perhaps Tate's most important contact with the agrarian wing of the Catholic Revival came when he renewed his acquaintance with lay activist Dorothy Day. A friend from their Greenwich Village period, Day had known Tate and Caroline Gordon before her conversion to Roman Catholicism in 1927. She associated with them when they were displaced southerners struggling to begin literary careers in New York City. In fact, she once lived across the street from the building where the Tates occupied a cold-water flat in exchange for Allen's modest services as janitor.[104] One of her autobiographical works, *The Long Loneliness*, mentions Tate as a "southern traditionalist" who shared the decentralist and anti-industrialist views of her southern-born lover, Forster Batterham.[105] For their part, the Tates remembered Day as an unconventional journalist with radical political sympathies—the pre-conversion Dorothy Day later obscured by Day and her admiring biographers. With fellow bohemians Malcolm Cowley and Eugene O'Neill, they knew the "wild" Day, who gained a reputation for, among other things, her ability to beat the "gangsters" of New York's Hell Hole saloon in drinking contests.[106]

In 1936, just prior to establishing Maryfarm, the first Catholic Worker agricultural commune, Day met with the Tates while Allen was teaching at Southwestern University in Memphis, Tennessee. Completing a tour of the upper South to advocate the organization of tenant farmers, she wanted to renew her relationship with the man who had defended American agriculture in *I'll Take My Stand*.[107] Later, Day functioned as a concrete example of "lost-generation" Catholic spirituality for the couple. In the 1950s, after their own conversions, they frequently visited St. Joseph's House of Hospitality, the Catholic Worker community in New York. Tate donated clothing to the Workers, and Gordon became especially attached to Day.[108] She even used Day as the model for the Catherine Pollard character in her 1956 novel *The Malefactors*—a book that greatly disturbed Day because of its frank portrayal of the young woman's sexual and religious experimentation.[109]

Enthusiastic over their meeting in 1936, Tate wrote to a Southern Agrarian colleague about Day and the "remarkable" *Catholic Worker* newspaper: "The editor…is greatly excited by our whole program.…A very remarkable woman. Terrific energy, much practical sense, and a fanatical devotion to the cause of the land!"[110] Tate's conversation with Day only confirmed the course his thought had been taking since his return from Europe. Within months of the meeting, he was even ready to use the *Catholic Worker* as the model for his own agrarian journal.[111] Just as the Southern Agrarian movement was beginning to wither, Tate encountered a modern Catholicism socially active, politically vibrant, historically grounded, and intellectually stimulating.

4 | Philosophy for a Christian Humanism

A man who finds his way to Catholicism, out of the tangle of modern culture and complexity, must think harder than he has ever thought in his life.

—G. K. Chesterton[1]

Catholicism appeals, no longer to the antiquarian faddist or to the restless in search of spiritual adventure, but to the lovers of order. It beckons like a life-boat to shipwrecked souls who have seen the conventions go down under their feet.

—Ronald Knox[2]

Already Catholic in spirit by the 1930s, Allen Tate successfully resisted the urge to convert for a number of years. To the Catholic Poetry Society, he represented himself as "a Protestant, or let me say a non-Catholic, writer who happens to be intensely sympathetic towards the Catholic tradition."[3] Yet still he hesitated to embrace that tradition completely and publicly. At the time, he was keenly aware that, in the world of letters, Catholicism continued to have a bad reputation for stifling creative writing. As Ronald Knox had observed, outsiders saw conversion to the faith as a form of "intellectual suicide."[4] Like C. S. Lewis, however, Tate learned that a "man who wishes to remain a sound Atheist cannot be too careful of his reading." For Lewis, danger came in the form of Chesterton's *Everlasting Man*, a crucial text in his journey from unbelief to Christian theism.[5] For Tate, the works of the Thomistic revival became the texts of his intellectual conversion. Had Tate not discovered the enticing system of Neo-Thomism, his interest in Catholicism would have remained perverse spiritual flirtation.

Closely allied with the preconciliar church's agrarian movement, the novel intellectual synthesis of Neo-Thomism played a vital role in the Catholic Revival. The popes based their social teaching on it, and Catholic agrarians raised their anti-industrialism on it. According to the

72

National Catholic Rural Life Conference, the teachings of Thomas Aquinas provided the surest foundation for the Catholic philosophy of rural life.[6] One observer even described the English Distributist movement as a case of "applied Thomism."[7] Chesterton himself pointed to Thomism's contemporary impact on "a hundred crying questions of craftsmanship and ownership and economic ethics."[8] Indeed, it would be impossible to imagine the force of Catholicism's resistance to modernity or the fervor with which it defended the agrarian way of life without the modern assimilation of scholastic thought called Neo-Thomism.

William Halsey has characterized Neo-Thomism as a "philosophical structure of innocence," a facile instrument by which Catholics insulated their minds from the complexities of life between two world wars.[9] Challenging this thesis, Arnold Sparr has credited the revival of scholastic thought with sparking an "intellectual awakening" unparalleled in modern Catholic history. The modern appreciation of Aquinas provided the Catholic Revival with such impressive intellectual coherence that Calvert Alexander considered it the "official philosophy" of the literary flowering.[10] According to historian Patrick Carey, Neo-Thomism furnished "a satisfying intellectual framework" for realizing the aim of a restored Catholic culture.[11]

"The Golden Wisdom"

Allegiance to Neo-Thomism served as the intellectual shibboleth of the Catholic Revival. While not all Catholic writers of the time were convinced Thomists, the philosophy's categories provided the international Revival with a common technical vocabulary and the promise of methodological virtuosity. Its potential as an intellectual system encouraged Revival efforts in a staggering variety of fields, ranging from philosophical debate and scientific research to art criticism and political analysis. According to Gerald McCool, the proponents of Neo-Thomism envisioned nothing less than "the creation of a contemporary philosophy which, while taking its inspiration from the wisdom of the Angelic Doctor, would make its own contribution to the integration of European culture."[12] Receiving unlimited support from the church's magisterium, Neo-Thomism definitively shaped the intellectual world of the Catholic Revival.

Historians of the movement locate the origins of the Neo-Thomistic impulse in the intellectual ferment of the period just prior to the First Vatican Council (1869–1870).[13] Since the sixteenth-century Council of Trent, the church had juggled an unwieldy pluralism in its efforts to defend and propagate the truths of Catholic belief. After a brief resurgence of scholasticism in the late sixteenth and early seventeenth centuries, Catholic thought accommodated itself to an intellectual agenda set by the secular Enlightenment. As Yves Congar has stated, the Catholic theology of the Tridentine era sought its foundations "not in the Christian tradition of Augustine, Thomas Aquinas, and Bonaventure, but in the miscellaneous philosophies, which by turn had their day in the sun."[14] In the nineteenth century, critics of the status quo found the Catholic mind in disturbing disarray. Alarmed by the inadequacy of Catholic responses to Enlightenment rationalism and post-Enlightenment romanticism, Catholic restorationists yearned for a common system that would rescue Catholics from uncritical eclecticism and the increasingly sectarian character of modern philosophy. Their calls for the unification of Catholic intellectual life paved the way for a church-sponsored revival of scholastic thought.

Especially dissatisfied with attempts to draft Cartesian philosophy into the service of Catholic doctrine, some European theologians agitated for an official endorsement of the thought and methods of thirteenth-century theologian Thomas Aquinas. Two Jesuit writers, Italian Matteo Liberatore and his German confrere Joseph Kleutgen, emerged as early leaders in the movement to grant a privileged place to scholastic thought. Their works, especially Liberatore's series of articles in the journal *Civiltà cattolica*, begun in 1853, and Kleutgen's five-volume *Die Theologie der Vorzeit* (1853–1870), pictured an updated Thomism as the only system capable of avoiding the metaphysical and epistemological errors of Descartes, Kant, Hegel, and the other doctors of modernity. Backed by powerful members of the Roman hierarchy, their efforts came to fruition in the first major encyclical of the pontificate of Leo XIII. Just as his *Rerum novarum* became the landmark of modern Catholic social teaching, Leo's *Aeterni patris* (1879) gave authoritative definition to what eventually became known as Neo-Thomism. In the document, Leo exhorted the bishops of the world to "restore the golden wisdom of St. Thomas, and to spread it far and wide for the defense and beauty of the Catholic faith, for the good of society, and for the advantage of all the sciences."[15]

After *Aeterni patris*, the church functioned as the patron of Thomistic trends in Catholic intellectual life. It struck what one critic has called "an exclusive contract" with neo-scholasticism and its attendant world view.[16] The implications of this relationship were most acutely felt in institutions geared toward the education of priests. In the form of textbooks, commentaries, and Latin manuals, scholasticism saturated seminary learning. Catholic colleges, universities, and faculties of theology also submitted to Thomistic reform. The Gregorian University in Rome, for example, served as a bastion of neo-scholasticism. Likewise, Desire Mercier established Belgium's University of Louvain as a distinguished center for Neo-Thomistic scholarship. Other notable institutions in the new Thomistic network included Fribourg, Innsbruck, the Institut Catholique of Paris, and the French Dominican school of Le Saulchoir at Kain. In the United States, the Catholic University of America patterned its curriculum according to the Thomistic vision, as did other universities such as the Jesuit schools Marquette University and Saint Louis University. Gradually, professional societies and international study centers dedicated to Thomism provided an infrastructure for the renovated world of Catholic thought. By the first decades of the twentieth century, new scholarly journals began to extend the influence of Neo-Thomism. The *Revue Thomiste* and *Revue Neo-Scolastique* prevailed on the European scene, as the *Thomist, Thought, New Scholasticism,* and *Modern Schoolman* brought the movement into libraries and classrooms across America.

Especially after the condemnation of modernism in 1907, Thomism became virtually synonymous with theological orthodoxy. Pius X reaffirmed Leo's verdict on Thomism in his antimodernist *Pascendi.* "Scholastic philosophy," he declared, must "be made the basis of the sacred sciences."[17] In *Doctoris angelici* (1914), he continued to emphasize the centrality of Thomism in Roman Catholic thought. To mark the six hundredth anniversary of the canonization of Aquinas, Pius XI issued the pro-scholastic *Studiorum ducem* (1923). Eight years later, his apostolic constitution, *Deus scientiarum,* promoted the "integration of Catholic higher teaching around the *Summa.*"[18] Finally, Pius XII's encyclical *Humani generis* (1950), while gingerly admitting scholasticism's limitations, warned against novelties in the church's theological enterprise. "As we well know from the experience of centuries," the letter confidently reasserted, "the method of Aquinas is singularly preeminent both for teaching students and for bringing truth to light."[19] According to Congar, writing near mid-century, modern Catholic theology developed solely "under the aegis of St. Thomas and Scholastic philosophy."[20]

Briefly put, modern Thomism emphasized the following themes: the reliability of human reason, the dependence of mental operations upon sense experience, the compatibility of reason with divine revelation, the complementary relation of supernatural grace to nature, and the symbiotic relationship of philosophy with theology. Rooting its program in the "common sense," moderate realism of Aristotelian metaphysics, it deplored the ideological fragmentation of the sciences and dreamed of the future reunification of all academic disciplines devoted to the unity

of truth. By definition, it assumed that medieval scholasticism represented the golden age of Catholic intellectual activity, that the achievement of Aquinas typified the high point of that period, and that
Thomism ultimately could be reconciled with other scholastic theologies.
The hallmark of the movement, of course, was the belief that Thomism
possessed a peculiarly timeless quality, enabling it to speak to the most
modern of issues. Writing for the first *Catholic Encyclopedia*, Louvain's
medieval historian, the layman Maurice de Wulf, explained that neo-
scholasticism was "not merely the resuscitation of a philosophy long
since defunct, but rather a restatement in our own day of the *philosophia
perennia*."[21] In this respect, as David Tracy has noted, Neo-Thomism
resembled other twentieth-century theologies constructed according to
the Neo-Orthodox paradigm.[22] Opponents of the movement criticized
what they perceived as Neo-Thomism's lack of historical consciousness,
its failure to grasp modern cognitional theories, its refusal to deal adequately with nagging hermeneutical problems, and its tendency to
equate Thomistic conclusions with the data of Christian revelation.

In contemporary opinion, the modern Thomistic revival often bears
the stigma of a static, monolithic, and inflexible approach to theological issues, a system of rigid order and intellectual retrenchment.
Recently, however, some scholars have attempted to investigate the
dynamic, internal varieties of twentieth-century Neo-Thomism, explor-
ing what one participant in the movement, French philosopher Etienne
Gilson, called Thomism's "big family."[23] George Huntston Williams, for
example, has identified three main thrusts within the movement: (1)
the traditional Thomism of Jacques Maritain and Dominican priest
Reginald Garrigou-Lagrange, utilizing the classical scholastic commentaries; (2) the transcendental Thomism of Joseph Maréchal (and later,
Karl Rahner and Bernard Lonergan), concerned with formulating a
Thomism responsive to the challenges of post-Kantian work in epistemology; and (3) the existential or historical Thomism of Gilson, concentrating on the Aquinas revealed by historical research and on the
primacy of being in his Christian philosophy.[24] Like all large families,
Neo-Thomism gave rise to many intricately interrelated branches.
Unfortunately, when the movement has not been completely ignored by
intellectual historians, studies have typically focused on the ecclesiastical wing of the family, using "Neo-Thomism" to refer exclusively to the
uninspiring handbooks of clerical training, the official documents of
Vatican authorities, or the purely academic research of Catholic theological faculties. With the exception of William Halsey's work, no study
has adequately treated the full cultural history of Neo-Thomism
beyond the borders of officially Roman Catholic institutions. Catholic

historiography is just beginning to take stock of what Chesterton viewed as Aquinas' "startling" reappearance "in the current culture of the colleges and the salons."[25]

While papal encyclicals and catechetical books had their place, the Thomism of the Catholic Revival derived mainly from the cosmopolitan Neo-Thomism of the great lay philosophers of the period. The works of Maritain and Gilson enjoyed phenomenal popularity among the educated laity of the day. Overlooking technical points of intramural rivalry, Revival proponents gained from them a sense of intellectual mission in the modern world. They appropriated wholesale Maritain's convictions regarding St. Thomas as the "Apostle of our time" and his system as a "missionary philosophy." At the same time, they ratified his pronouncement of Aquinas as "our predestined guide in the reconstruction of Christian culture."[26] Unlike the scholasticism of the seminaries, the Revival's Neo-Thomism communicated a vibrant vision of Catholic philosophy's cultural mission. Rarely fixating on minute points of philosophical detail, lay Catholic elites used Thomism's adroit mediation between sacred and secular to engage modern thinkers on pressing questions of society, art, and politics. In fact, Gilson and Maritain found extraordinarily receptive audiences on the secular campuses of North American colleges and universities. Dating the true beginning of the movement from her husband's 1913 lectures at the Institut Catholique of Paris, Raissa Maritain described how this Thomism was "claiming its rights in profane life and culture, entering the lists with contemporary philosophies, entering into competition with them on their own grounds, as young and even more alive than the doctrines of the day."[27] In interdisciplinary scholarship, popular pamphlets, and even historical novels and children's books, this "creative" or "living" Thomism infused Catholic Revival enthusiasts with the intellectual resources they thought necessary for cultural revitalization.[28] Thomas Aquinas was their contemporary, they said, and their vocation was to "carry the light" of his doctrine "to all the problems of our times, to widen its frontiers...[and] to reinsert it into the existential reality of the movement of culture and philosophy."[29]

"Dispossessed and Forlorn Orthodoxy"

Writing of the fertile period in his intellectual life, between his 1906 conversion and his discovery of Aquinas around 1908, Maritain observed, "I was already a Thomist without knowing it."[30] The same may have been true of Allen Tate. In his personal recollection of Tate, literary critic Walter Sullivan has maintained that "Allen had been a neo-Scholastic and therefore an Aristotelian before he had become a Catholic."[31] While hardly a consistent thinker trained in matters of philosophical method, Tate did demonstrate an early predilection for Aristotelian metaphysics, much of which was inherited from his classically minded teacher and colleague John Crowe Ransom. His early essays for the *Sewanee Review* on "Poetry and the Absolute" (1927) and "Confusion and Poetry" (1930) clearly revealed this tendency, and Richard Foster documented it twenty years before Sullivan.[32] But a taste for Aristotle or Aquinas does not necessarily impel one toward the baptismal font. The legacy of University of Chicago philosopher Mortimer Adler, the perennial philosophy's greatest Jewish advocate, stands as a persuasive witness against such snap judgments. For his part, Tate admitted that "it is difficult to detect the exact moment of conversion."[33] He knew that "the roads to genuine belief" were many, and that the process of conversion led one into ultimate mystery. Whether or not Aristotle provided the initial motivation, Tate was not prepared to say. He only recognized the fact that his experience was a case of "the progress from intellectual to intuitive belief."[34]

When Newman attempted to trace the course of the "great revolution of mind" that led him to the Roman Catholic Church, he marveled at the complexity of the process called religious conversion. In his *Apologia Pro Vita Sua*, he wrote, "Who can know himself, and the multitude of subtle influences which act upon him?"[35] Nearly a century later, several factors converged in the experience of Allen Tate, each contributing its force to the shape of a mental revolution comparable to Newman's. Some worked on the level of his intellectual sensibilities; others on the plane of personal influences; still others on deeper and less accessible levels of consciousness. All of them, however, engaged what Newman called the concrete being. Together, they made Tate more than simply another critic of modernity partial to the least modern of the Christian churches.

The conversion of his protégé, poet Robert "Cal" Lowell, in 1941, followed by that of Caroline Gordon six years later, arguably moved Tate closer to formal affiliation with the Roman Catholic Church. Since Lowell and his wife, writer Jean Stafford, lived with the Tates immediately after Lowell's entrance into the church, Tate had the opportunity to observe the convert's religion firsthand. Unfortunately Lowell's Catholicism veered toward an irritating form of modern Jansenism, breeding only gnostic fanaticism and a self-righteous priggishness. For him, Roman Catholic faith required intellectual intolerance and scrupulous observance of ritual, as well as, evidently, renunciation of marital relations. Hoping to merge poetic vocation and religious faith in a career with the Catholic publishing firm Sheed and Ward, he went so far as to fantasize about sacrificing all literary aspirations for an apostolate with the Catholic Workers or the street-corner apologists of the Catholic Evidence Guild.[36] In a letter of paternal concern, John Crowe Ransom warned Lowell against basing everything on the assumption that "Thomism makes for human happiness."[37] Gordon, on the other hand, showed Tate a healthier brand of Catholic conversion. Like the romantic Lowell, she enjoyed "all the trappings of Catholicism" in addition to the intellectual discipline of the spiritual classics. From the beginning, though, her faith took a domestic and more levelheaded turn, eventually becoming fully integrated into her family life and art.[38]

Of considerable importance to Tate's conversion, moreover, was his association with Princeton University beginning in 1939. As poet in residence there, he came under the influence of what Gerald McCool has called the "second stage" of twentieth-century neo-scholasticism.[39] Specifically, Tate's encounter and ensuing friendship with the distinguished visiting professor Jacques Maritain provided him with the personal model and public language he required for full acceptance of the Catholic faith. As Tate himself later put it, "Jacques Maritain's influence on me was pervasive from the time I first knew him."[40]

Apparently, Tate and Maritain met during the latter's first extended stay in the United States. Living in New York, Maritain taught occasionally at Princeton during the years of his Second World War exile. Later, after serving as postwar France's ambassador to the Vatican, he returned to the university to offer philosophy courses from 1948 to 1960. In 1949, the Tates moved to Benbrackets, their home on Princeton's Nassau Street, just a few blocks from the Maritains' Mediterranean-style home on Linden Lane. Residing within comfortable walking distance of St. Paul's church, the sole Roman Catholic parish in "Presbyterian" Princeton, both couples entered into a close relationship of mutual friendship.[41] If Dorothy Day had shown Tate how a "lost-generation" bohemian could embrace Roman Catholicism, Maritain personified for him the ideal of the Catholic "man of letters." Respected scholar, Vatican statesman, and Christian gentleman, Maritain gave exquisite testimony to the lay intellectual's potential in the Catholic Church. Profoundly affected by Maritain's thought and personality, Tate also exerted an influence on the elder philosopher. Assigning Tate a place among the great writers of the American canon, Maritain generously quoted from Tate's poetry and prose in his magisterial *Creative Intuition in Art and Poetry* (1953) and mentioned him favorably in his *Reflections on America* (1958).[42] Perhaps the Maritains' greatest tribute to their American friend came when they translated into French his "Ode to the Confederate Dead."[43]

Even before his encounter with Maritain, T. S. Eliot's *Criterion* thrust Tate the reluctant unbeliever into the midst of Thomism's growing international family. According to Russell Kirk, Eliot functioned as the voice of what Santayana once called "a dispossessed and forlorn orthodoxy" in the modern world.[44] In its thirteen years of existence, from 1922 to 1935, his journal emerged as the privileged instrument for that orthodoxy, often rendering its voice in distinctly Thomistic accents. Scorned by some critics for "its intellectualism, its traditionalism, and its devotion to 'lost causes,'" *Criterion* represented for Tate a stubborn standard of civilization in an age of cultural disorder.[45] When Tate submitted to the journal his essay on "The Fallacy of Humanism," he joined the ranks of Thomism's fellow travelers.

An admirer of Maritain since 1925, Eliot opened the pages of *Criterion* to the writers of the Catholic Intellectual Renaissance, Roman and Anglican. The journal featured articles by Henri Massis, Douglas Jerrold, Evelyn Underhill, Charles Maurras, and Christopher Dawson. It devoted the issues of an entire year to a prolonged discussion of Action Française. It also reviewed a steady flow of books by Belloc, Chesterton, Knox, Gill, and Hollis, and documents from Pope Pius XI. A literary quarterly boasting no specialized philosophical credentials, the journal became one of the best forums for modern Thomistic explorations in religion and culture. Maritain's analysis of "Poetry and Religion" and Martin D'Arcy's articulation of "The Thomistic Synthesis and Intelligence" represented the first major forays of neo-scholasticism outside the parochial boundaries of ecclesiastical and academic circles.[46] The journal regularly reviewed the publications of both Thomists, and Gilson's work also received sympathetic criticism. Like Seward Collins' *Bookman*, the journal forged alliances between Neo-Thomists and other defenders of Western culture outside the Catholic Church.

Surrounded by Christian and non-Christian Neo-Thomists, Tate appreciated the promise of Thomism as a coherent intellectual system. He even recognized the rise of Neo-Thomism as a "fundamental" issue that all critical journals had to engage.[47] In 1944, as editor of the newly revived *Sewanee Review*, housed on the campus of Tennessee's University of the South, Tate invited Maritain to contribute an article for the inaugural issue on "the relation of Christianity to contemporary literature."[48] Soon after the appearance of the *Thomist*'s special Maritain volume in 1943, Tate began to study Maritain's works in earnest, beginning with *The Dream of Descartes* in English translation. By 1948, Tate exercised a reasonable fluency in the grammar of Thomistic thought and could negotiate his way, as an amateur Christian philosopher, through complex arguments in metaphysics and epistemology. No longer hesitant, he took instructions and prepared himself for baptism.

"There Could Be a Place"

Tate's appropriation of the Catholic Revival's Thomistic philosophy coincided with the rise of the literary movement called New Criticism, the mid-century academic success story in Anglo-American literary theory.[49] An approach to literary analysis famous for its emphasis on a formalist interpretation of texts, New Criticism captured the momentum begun by early twentieth-century theorists I. A. Richards and T. E. Hulme. In the aftermath of the Southern Agrarian crusade, already losing steam by the mid-1930s, members of the original symposium, primarily writers by training, returned to more literary pursuits. Ransom, for example, left the South, accepted a position at Ohio's Kenyon College, and all but renounced his involvement in "the agrarian nostalgia"—what he later called "the last fling of our intellectual youth."[50] Once the unofficial dean of the movement, he felt that the crusade had turned too political. Concerned about Agrarianism's effect on the purity of their literary careers, he complained to Tate that "*patriotism* is eating at *lyricism*."[51] Later, even Tate confessed that the Agrarian preoccupation with the Old South amounted to a "theological problem," the illicit worship of a "perishable god."[52]

Attempting to retain the creative edge of his Agrarianism in an enlarged campaign of cultural criticism, Tate gained fresh recognition for his accomplishments in New Criticism. Works such as *Reason in Madness* (1941) and *On the Limits of Poetry* (1948) established him as a premier figure in the American branch of the movement, along with former Agrarians Ransom, Cleanth Brooks, and Robert Penn Warren. In these collections of essays, Tate continued to lace his defense of *avant-garde* modern literature with a traditionalist polemic against modern society. He also endorsed New Criticism's call for an "ontological" criticism. Affirming a form of real knowledge by means of the concrete literary image, distinct from that obtained through rational, scientific cognition, this type of criticism echoed traditional points of Aristotelian literary theory. Consequently, it made New Criticism attractive to English departments in Catholic colleges and universities across America. Often decried for its erudite classicism, its endorsement of the idea of a hierarchy of values, and its apparent sanction of traditional authority, New Criticism suffered the opposition of critics who labeled it "an odd blending of fascist politics and aesthetic formalism."[53] Some detected in the movement an absolutism strangely akin to Roman Catholic doctrine.[54]

Though other New Critics turned for metaphysical support to the aesthetic theory of Immanuel Kant or the Protestant Neo-Orthodoxy of Reinhold Niebuhr, Tate capitalized on New Criticism's apparent similarities to Catholic thought. He infused his criticism with philosophical resources borrowed from Neo-Thomism. In the summer of 1950, in an *American Scholar* forum, Tate made a revealing reply to the accusation that New Critics advocated a reactionary dogmatism at variance with the spirit of American democracy:

> I am not a Catholic, but I would like to feel that there could be a place where an intelligent Catholic might publish criticism in this country....I don't say that the Catholic literary critics ought to capture the scene. But why can't an American who happens to be a Catholic espouse an authoritarian tradition in religion and exhibit it for what it's worth, put it into currency and let it take its chances with other points of view?[55]

Within a matter of months after those remarks, Tate was himself that intelligent American Catholic striving to articulate religious criticism informed by a Catholic vision.

Encouraged by his godparents, Jacques and Raissa Maritain, Tate received baptism on 22 December, the feast day of Thomas the "doubting" Apostle. In accordance with the conventions of the time, the ceremony, conducted at the Benedictine priory of St. Mary's in rural New Jersey, was a private and modest affair. Just over an hour's drive from the Princeton campus, St. Mary's functioned as something of a haven for intellectual converts while Father Hugh Duffy presided as prior of the community from 1947 to 1952. Because the monks rarely performed baptisms at the priory, Tate's rite of initiation was officially registered at St. Margaret's church in nearby Morristown. In May of the next year, Tate received the sacrament of confirmation, taking the name of Augustine. Subsequently, his family (including his adult daughter Nancy, her husband Percy Wood, and their children) became registered members of St. Paul's church.[56] Maritain compared Tate to the fifth-century Frankish king Clovis, whose conversion brought a nation into the church.[57]

The literary world responded to the news of Tate's conversion with generosity and optimism. Donald Davidson, putting aside his strident anticlericalism, assured his friend that he could understand his attraction to "the Mother Church."[58] William Lynch, the Jesuit editor of *Thought*, relayed his certainties regarding Tate's vocation in the church.[59] The Who's Who of the Revival, *Catholic Authors*, hurried a biographical sketch of Tate into print,[60] and the former president of the Catholic Poetry Society, herself a convert, introduced *Catholic World* readers to the Revival's newest "paradoxical pilgrim."[61] Likewise, Bernetta Quinn, the Franciscan literary scholar at Minnesota's College of St. Teresa, confessed her joy over Tate's entrance into "the Mystical Body" of the Catholic Church.[62]

Ransom saved his response for the *Sewanee Review*'s celebration of Tate's sixtieth birthday. In a glowing tribute to his erstwhile student, he expressed empathy for Tate's decision. "Religion is so imperative for a society," he said, "that those of us who do not profess it are glad when our friends do." Praising Tate for a lifetime of literary achievement, he also expressed the sentiment that many others would harbor at one time or another:

> Allen would have been a theologian and a poet in [the] Middle Ages when there was a sort of closure of the whole mind under the religious prescription....He found a world order more to his purpose in a Church which has an imperial name, and retains from the Middle Ages its immensely careful yet liberal Scholastic theology.[63]

Huck Finn in Rome

Apparently the urbane man of letters long awaited by Catholic America, the convert Tate anxiously sought to define the nature of his apostolate in the church. He expanded his circle of acquaintances in the Catholic community and enlarged his already burdensome correspondence to include an impressive number of leading Catholic writers, editors, publishers, educators, and scholars. His papers, housed in Princeton University's Firestone Library, contain scores of letters from a variety of significant Catholic personalities, representing all aspects of the Catholic Revival. Including brief notes from figures such as Belloc, François Mauriac, and Julian Green, the collection demonstrates Tate's intentional efforts to build relationships with influential Catholic intellectuals after 1950. In addition to Maritain and his spiritual director Father Marion Casey, lay theologian Frank Sheed, writer Graham Greene, and Jesuit intellectuals Martin D'Arcy, Walter Ong, and William Lynch joined Tate's group of regular correspondents and confidants.

Tate's conversion also enhanced the character of the many speaking engagements and editorial commitments that shaped his erratic career. America's religious media wasted no time in approaching Tate with a variety of plans for his involvement in religious publishing and broadcasting. The Jesuit journal of comment, *America*, and the Lutheran *Salt* solicited articles on American letters, while *A.D.* magazine, the self-styled vehicle for a modern spiritual renaissance, offered him a position as contributing editor. Similarly, students at the Roman Catholic University of Dallas hoped Tate would contribute to their periodical, *Kerygma*. Aside from print journalism, the National Council of Catholic Men attempted to secure Tate's presence as a guest on the CBS television program "Light Unto My Feet."[64]

In similar fashion, numerous church-related colleges and universities invited Tate to lecture on their campuses. Catholic schools such as Fordham, Loyola, Creighton, Webster, Bellarmine, St. John's (Collegeville), St. Mary's (Notre Dame), Newton College of the Sacred Heart, and St. Mary-of-the-Woods inundated him with letters, seeking the presence of the eminent convert. Boston College slated him to deliver the Candlemas Lectures for 1951. In 1952, the College of St. Thomas in Minnesota invited him to deliver the annual Archbishop Ireland Lecture on "Catholicism and Modern Literature."[65] The next year, following the recommendation of a committee including George Shuster, Vernon Bourke, and John Courtney Murray, Marquette University nominated Tate to be the Catholic Educational Association's Gabriel Richard Lecturer. Some institutions, such as the University of Notre Dame and Newman College at the University of Melbourne, Australia, negotiated with Tate regarding temporary assignments as a visiting professor. Others contemplated more elaborate arrangements. After bestowing upon him the Christian Culture Award, previously given to Frank Sheed, Assumption University in Windsor, Ontario, even considered creating for Tate a chair in Christian Humanism and Culture.[66]

Though he declined a number of the offers, the years during which he received most of these invitations, roughly between 1951 and 1958, marked the high watermark of Tate's Catholic experience. Already well known outside the United States, he fast became a member of the international Catholic lecture scene. After accepting his only tenured academic position (on the English faculty of the University of Minnesota), he spent much of his time traveling to a variety of foreign countries, acting as something of a self-appointed world ambassador of Christian humanism. He addressed the Congress of Cultural Freedom in Paris, the United Nations Educational, Scientific, and Cultural Organization (UNESCO) in Venice, and the Congress for Peace and Christian

Civilization in Florence. As a Fulbright professor, he lectured at Oxford University and the American Academy in Rome. Between formal engagements, he participated in retreats for Catholic laymen at Eau Vive in Paris, attended prayers at Blackfriars near Oxford, went to Mass at the church of St. Thomas the Apostle in Bombay, India, and aggressively studied the Catholic intellectual tradition. In addition to the contemporary works of Maritain, Gilson, Martin D'Arcy, Walter Ong, Romano Guardini, and Fulton Sheen, he read widely in patristic, medieval, and Counter-Reformation classics. The sixteenth-century Spanish mystic John of the Cross became a particular favorite. "Like Huck Finn," Tate wrote with mock humility, "I find the words tough, but I am getting into it. I shall never be a mystic, but in spite of that his doctrine is the pattern of the spiritual life, the lower stages of which are within our reach."[67]

Tate's correspondence during these years indicates that for the first time, he viewed Europe through the eyes of a religious pilgrim. He visited an assortment of monasteries, churches, and reliquaries, one year attending Easter and Ascension liturgies at St. Peter's Basilica in Rome. He read the Little Office, went to confession regularly, and, when possible, assisted at daily Mass. Stephen Spender's photograph of a reverent Tate, standing by an Italian roadside shrine dedicated to the Virgin Mary, pictures the convert in his finest hour.[68] Undoubtedly Tate's greatest honor in the first years of his Catholic experience came when he had the opportunity to meet Pope Pius XII in August of 1952. In Rome, before the UNESCO meeting, Tate used Maritain's contacts with Vatican officials to his advantage. Like many intellectual converts, Tate found Pius' brand of Europeanism, anticommunism, and ascetic spirituality an appealing mix. In the aftermath of the 1950 pilgrimage year and in anticipation of the upcoming Marian Year, the postwar popularity of Pius XII had never been higher, especially given the circulation of rumors about the Vatican's recent discovery of St. Peter's bones. In a touching letter to Caroline Gordon, Tate described his private audience at Castel Gandolfo, the pope's summer villa. Studying "the noblest human face I've ever seen," he said, "I was so scared that my knees shook." Evidently, Tate had originally planned to discuss with Pius all the problems of the American church, but the language barrier between the two men and the fact that Tate had forgotten his notes in his hurried response to the Vatican messenger summoning him to the audience prevented the writer from having more than a superficial conversation with the pontiff.[69] Before the audience was over, though, he regained his confidence, asking Pius for a blessing on "American Catholic men of letters."[70]

Tate's request for an apostolic blessing on American Catholic writers revealed the current shape of an idea that he had been nursing for a while. During this period, a specific issue that concerned him was the need to foster a greater sense of community among lay Catholic intellectuals. Dating back to his involvement with the Fugitives and the Southern Agrarians, as well as his fascination with Action Française, Tate displayed a strong interest in the communal dimensions of the intellectual life. The idea of a "republic of letters," in fact, functioned as a constant in his evolving set of cultural values. The Maritains, too, entertained visions of clusters of Catholic thinkers and artists devoted to the advance of Christian culture. Their homes in Meudon, New York, and Princeton became locations famous for their warmth of Christian fellowship and their spirit of interdisciplinary dialogue. They especially dreamed of establishing a *cercle d'etudes thomistes*, a spiritual fraternity that would unite intellectuals from all scientific specializations in dedication to the thought of Thomas Aquinas.[71]

Dissatisfied with the activist posture of the elite Committee of Catholics for Cultural Action, which prized the membership of eminent lay Catholic intellectuals, Tate made various attempts to organize an alternative academy of Catholic writers that would promote Catholic values in society without endorsing a specifically political agenda.[72] One such plan called for the establishment of a school of writing "in a Catholic atmosphere," modeled after Péguy's Entretiens de Pontigny of prewar France. Naming it "Conversations at Newburgh," Tate arranged to house the academy's facilities at Dorothy Day's Maryfarm in the New York Hudson Valley.[73] Redefining his old Agrarian commitment in terms of restoring "humane life" based on "the order of a unified Christendom,"[74] he announced the purpose of the new project as the propagation of a "far-reaching philosophy for a Catholic humanism."[75]

"Theories from the Thomistic Revival"

All students of Tate's work agree that Catholic humanism, specifically preconciliar Thomism, harmonized resourcefully with his developing views of culture and tradition. It honored, as Gale Carrithers has put it, "intellect even while insisting on its limitations in a fallen world."[76] Critical opinion divides, however, when it comes to evaluating the nature of Thomism's impact on Tate's work. Recognizing that his poetic productivity gradually declined after his conversion, Radcliffe Squires, Robert Brinkmeyer, and Robert Dupree have nevertheless credited Tate's internalization of Catholic faith with some of his most profound insights. For example, they have ranked "Seasons of the Soul" (1944) and the trilogy of "The Maimed Man" (1952), "The Swimmers" (1953), and "The Buried

Lake" (1953) among Tate's greatest poems.[77] By contrast, Paul Giles has squarely blamed "ingenious but archaic theories from the Thomistic revival" for alleged didactic and apologetic tones in Tate's later prose writings. According to him, Tate fell victim to the very temptation he tried so hard to avoid. He "mastered the teachings of Catholicism just too carefully," Giles claims, ultimately sacrificing critical discernment to the gods of religious orthodoxy.[78] In other words, what Knox said about intellectual suicide may have been right on target.

With such a range of opinion, it is easy to divide Tate's interpreters into two opposing camps: those who believe Catholic thought exercised a positive effect on his work, and those who attribute to it a detrimental effect. Unfortunately, the debate, framed in this manner, is guilty of the fallacy of intention, granting Tate's philosophical and religious beliefs causal control over his creative abilities—the very fate, of course, that he himself had feared prior to conversion. Furthermore, it may be responsible for what approximates a conspiracy of silence in the critical literature regarding Tate's self-image as a Catholic critic. Whether or not it hindered his muse, Tate himself thought that Catholic humanism, as expressed in Thomism, raised his work to a new level of intellectual clarity and confidence.

Given Tate's self-conscious adoption of the identity of a Catholic critic, an appropriated Neo-Thomism must be seen not as an accidental element of his work, but as the substantial force animating his long-term critical project. In fact, from Tate's perspective, Neo-Thomism perfected his aim in criticism. His main critical writings of the decade after his conversion reveal how Thomism provided the integrative interpretive paradigm capable of unifying his literary and social criticism. Specifically, it enabled him to isolate, with an accuracy never before possible, what he perceived to be the principal crisis of his age. During his involvement in the Southern Agrarian movement, of course, Tate had gained a reputation in modernist circles as a fervent opponent of intellectual activity divorced from meaningful absorption in a concrete tradition of shared life and language. After his conversion to Roman Catholicism, he intensified his campaign against this "unliteral imagination."[79] As a strategic step in his project, he relied upon the Neo-Thomistic analogical imagination to furnish the metaphysical warrants for his judgments in moral criticism. The traditional doctrines of the "analogy of being" and the "analogy of grace" furnished Tate with basic principles that ratified his New Critical hunches regarding the complex relation of readers to texts, of citizens to culture, of humans to nature, and of creatures to their Creator. In short, he ordered his criticism according to what Gilson called "the sacramental character of the Christian universe."[80]

In his only novel, *The Fathers* (1938), Tate had already put the doctrine into the mind of the narrator:

> Our senses, not being mechanisms, actually perform the miracles of imagination that they themselves create: from our senses come the metaphors through which we know the world, and in turn our senses get knowledge of the world by means of figures of their own making.[81]

Later, with catechetical precision, Tate articulated the same principle in his own criticism:

> The human intellect cannot reach God as essence; only God as analogy. Analogy to what? Plainly analogy to the natural world; for there is nothing in the intellect that has not previously reached it through the senses.[82]

Stimulated by Thomism's apparently universal applicability, Tate dedicated much of his Catholic career to a critique of modernity's anxious flight into gnostic abstraction.

"The Social Function of the Writer"

More than the famous "close reading" that classroom shorthand often uses to summarize the method of the New Critics, Tate's brand of New Criticism was primarily distinguished by a heightened sense of the importance of concrete image, figurative language, and organic form in authentic literature. For him, as for his fellow New Critic Cleanth Brooks, meaning resided within the densely metaphorical texture of a text. "*Form is meaning*," declared the credo of New Criticism: "*The general and the universal are not seized upon by abstraction, but got at through the concrete and the particular*."[83] Tate's mature literary theory located the fundamental flaw of the modern imagination in its departure from what Erich Auerbach described as the mimetic representation of reality once dominant in the Western intellectual tradition.[84] Generously utilizing the Thomistic philosophy of Maritain to analyze modern literature's propensity toward varieties of philosophical dualism, Tate proposed as a corrective the imaginative recovery of what Ransom, following Aquinas, referred to as "the world's body."[85] For Tate, the redemption of modern poetry required rediscovering "the external world which by analogy could become the interior world of the mind."[86]

This conviction forced Tate to part company with the purists in New Criticism solely concerned with the intricate inner life of literary texts. In his major prose works of the period, Tate converted the literary principle of the analogical imagination into a broad program of religio-social criticism aimed at reversing what he once called Emerson's "great intellectual mistake."[87] Granting the nineteenth-century figure paradigmatic status, he detected in the Emersonian legacy the same thing that Maritain had found in the Cartesian heritage: a parlous "lust for pure spirituality," independent of things.[88] Like his young friend Flannery O'Connor, Tate linked this strain in American intellectual history to the origins of a subtle "vaporization of religion" in modern culture. Denying that the sacred "can be known anagogically or defined dogmatically or received sacramentally" (as O'Connor put it),[89] this legacy represented for Tate a severe impoverishment of the religious imagination, a prophetic mental gesture signaling modern religion's future course. With its suspicion of physical ritual, its dismissal of institutional church, and its scruples regarding corporeal symbol, it constituted for him nothing less than a modern resurgence of ancient gnosticism—a latter-day protest against the traditional assertion of classical Christian orthodoxy that revelation must seek material expression and religion public cultural embodiment.

Though at times he vigorously resisted the suggestion that writers have social responsibilities beyond those required by public language and private conscience, Tate's irrepressible concern for the fate of modern society overruled his theoretical conclusions regarding the limits of literary criticism. One could argue that "the social function of the writer" actually preoccupied Tate in the 1950s.[90] In fact, Tate's affinity for the prophetic mode is well known among his interpreters.[91] Taking his place with other critics of modernist culture, Tate attempted to wed New Criticism and Neo-Thomism into an instrument of social prophecy, capable of arresting modern society's perverse attraction to the values of the gnostic temperament. Using literary theory as a foundation for cultural critique, he promoted a vision of the critic's religious vocation as the advocate of "the body of this world" to counter the sterile abstractions of modernity.

Adversus Omnes Haereses

T. S. Eliot, who, according to Tate, "made Christianity respectable in the world of letters,"[92] drafted a "primer of modern heresy," in which he alluded with ironic approbation to Pius IX's infamous "Syllabus of Errors" condemning liberalism, progress, and modern civilization.[93] Tate, too, found heresy a useful heuristic device in his extra-literary criticism. Indeed, for the "priestly class" of the New Critics,[94] it was always a short step from talk of literary "heresy" to a quasi-theological concern for spiritual heterodoxy. In most cases, the "heresy" represented not so much deviation from formally established church doctrine as risky migration from the mythic verities of an incarnate God that had informed Western presuppositions regarding the proper ordering of human society for centuries. With Tate, though, the lines separating literary judgment and theological appraisal were often intentionally blurred.

For Tate, the heresy that epitomized the false spirituality of his age was a fashionable target in twentieth-century polemics. A remarkably flexible category in the mid-century theological lexicon, "gnosticism" became for Tate's century what "enthusiasm" had been for the eighteenth. Aside from a handful of existentialist and Jungian scholars of religion who tried to argue for the enduring relevance of historical gnosticism, most theologians of the century's middle decades used the term pejoratively and ahistorically, freely employing it to refer to dualistic errors in fields from Christology and ecclesiology to anthropology and ethics. Though it had enjoyed currency in English letters since Milton's age and had designated the subject matter of specific historical research since the Victorian period, the term gained new potency from the discovery of the celebrated ancient texts at Nag Hammadi in 1945. Most non-theologians like Tate, however, used "gnosticism" in ways relating only tangentially to the Coptic documents, forming their opinions on the issue even before the publication of Hans Jonas' once authoritative *The Gnostic Religion* (1958). Like the meta-historians of his generation—Oswald Spengler, Hilaire Belloc, and Eric Voegelin—Tate came to see "gnosticism" as a collective symbol for a variety of intellectual and social forces threatening classical Christian civilization. He used the term to describe not just a fringe movement menacing the early Christian church but a perennial enemy of authentic Christian faith and identity. In religious life, according to Tate, gnosticism bred dangerous attitudes of moral independence and spiritual superiority, often expressed in an individualism aloof from the ordinary authority of community and tradition as well as in a defiant iconoclasm identifying real Christianity with an other-worldly purity emancipated from the limitations of external expressions and fallible institutions. In social life, by extension, Tate feared the gnostic aspects of modern society's infatuation with progress, its cult of technological efficiency, its worship of the future, its merciless contempt for tradition, and its foolish attachment to utopian schemes. The quest for life without boundaries, meaning without ambiguity, and good without evil characterized for Tate the essence of the secularized gnostic imagination. At best, he saw gnosticism as the carrier of a cluster of qualities associated with what H. Richard Niebuhr defined as the classic Christ-against-culture pattern in Christian spirituality: self-righteousness, perfectionism, antinomianism, and sectarianism.[95] At worst, Tate thought gnosticism a sinister force jeopardizing the Christian church from within.

Tate's Catholic campaign against gnosticism was anticipated by his early critique of abstraction in the modern mind. Despite his initial endorsement of Eliot's "lost-generation" doctrine of a "dissociation of sensibility," describing the modern spirit in terms of a dysfunctional split between reason and emotion,[96] Tate's emerging quarrel with modernity largely focused on the tragic alienation of modern intellectuals from their natural and cultural environment, a quality he habitually associated with the dialectical interiority of the New England mind. The nineteenth-century Transcendentalists may have been "born with knives in their brain," as Emerson said,[97] but Tate observed in their spiritual anatomy a set of brains cut off from commerce with the realities of natural and historical experience. By extracting the individual self from the constraints of tradition, community, time, and nature, and projecting it into a privatized realm of ethereal perfection, Tate believed, Emerson had drained the spiritual drama from human experience and transformed New England's robust intellectual heritage into "a sip of cambric tea." In the end, the "Lucifer of Concord" appeared less like the promethean devil of *Paradise Lost* and more like the unfortunate angel of Laodicea's lukewarm church.[98]

The current literary sign of that abstraction, for Tate, was the squeamish attitude of modern critics toward "the full body of experience" in a work of poetry.[99] To him, the critics' nervous retreat into alien disciplines such as sociology and psychology, in search of legitimacy for their own vocation, amounted to an ironic "revolt against literature itself."[100] Nothing captured the irony better for Tate than the typical graduate student in literature, eager to understand Shakespeare through detailed research of Elizabethan legal documents and financial records but reluctant to engage in serious analysis of the text itself.

The broader cultural signification of that modern abstraction, Tate concluded, was the equally misguided attempt on the part of religion's defenders to justify religion to the modern intellect only in vague and general terms. John Dewey, for example, called for a "common faith" based upon the religious quality of human experience, but his "sense of the whole" had little to do with an identifiable tradition of faith, language, and memory. In fact, as he admitted, it denoted "nothing in the way of a specifiable entity, either institutional or as a system of beliefs."[101] Even the nation's mainline denominations, as Philip Lee has suggested, followed the gnostic trajectory "from the particular to the nebulous."[102] Just as Quentin Anderson identified the track of Emerson's "imperial self" as "the American flight from...the institutions and emotional dispositions of associated life,"[103] Tate observed in modern religion curious resistance to the communal breadth and formal requirements of traditional religion. In a theory of religion analogous to what Eliot had constructed for literature in "Tradition and the Individual Talent," Tate argued against the possibility of religious commitment disengaged from cultural and institutional embodiment. With obvious reference to Alfred North Whitehead, whose famous definition of religion had located the essence of religion in the "solitariness" of the private individual, Tate maintained that "religious values, being communicable and not what you do with your solitude, are not personal...you cannot have religion without a religion."[104]

Tate first articulated that argument in his debate with representatives from the movement in literary scholarship known as New Humanism. The Ivy League New Humanists, principally Harvard's Irving Babbitt and Princeton's Paul Elmer More, commanded much attention between the Great War and the Depression. Not to be confused with the philosophical naturalists who signed the 1933 *Humanist Manifesto* and formed the American Humanist Association, the New Humanists were a small coalition of literature scholars who gained international prestige for their attempt to shore up a collapsing classical tradition against the surging tide of modernism. Opposed to trends in scholarship and higher education that threatened to enshrine utilitarian "scientism" and romantic egalitarianism as the unquestionable orthodoxies of the age, the New Humanists defended unpopular notions of tradition, high culture, and a hierarchy of values. Their project was rooted in the conviction that the canon of great books in the Western intellectual tradition contained the vital spiritual resources for the future of civilization.[105]

From the perspective of a late-twentieth-century literary scene dominated by Marxism, feminism, and multiculturalism, Tate's project appears roughly comparable to the New Humanists' kind of moral criticism. Both traditions have been eclipsed by the postmodernist turn in criticism, and neither has been able to shake the reputation of elitism. In the culture wars of the late 1920s, however, Tate engaged in a bit of intellectual sniping at the expense of the New Humanists. Concerned primarily with their sins of omission, Tate sought to demonstrate the extent of modern gnosticism's penetration into academic culture by exposing a level of modernist abstraction even in the reactionary strategies of the patrician New Humanists. While rightly contrasting the standards of the West's intellectual legacy with the "sham spirituality" of modern subjectivism,[106] the New Humanists, according to Tate, failed to appreciate the fact that the cherished values of Western culture obtained coherence only when based upon the systematic mythic structure of historical Christianity. The "pre-condition of all literature," Tate wrote, "is a body of mythology."[107] By contrast, "mere literature" without the reconstruction of a vital Christian civilization could not prevent the decay of Western culture.[108] Mocking the New Humanists for telling "us that Dante had values, but not how he got them," Tate asserted that "humanism is not enough...the background of an objective religion, a universal scheme of reference, is necessary."[109]

By the publication of *I'll Take My Stand* in 1930, Tate's critique had assumed its final pre-Catholic form. In the creed-like statement of principles preceding the volume's essays, the New Humanists were scored for treating humane culture as an "abstract system...derived from the classics," instead of "the whole way in which we live, act, think, and feel."[110] Tate's contribution itself advanced the thesis that no culture can flourish without what average citizens call institutional religion. Culture, he asserted, requires a specific religious structure organically informing its institutions and manners, for "abstraction is the death of religion."[111] Twenty years later, on the eve of his Catholic conversion, he continued to emphasize the point. Commenting on the so-called revival of religion among intellectuals after the Second World War, Tate warned against the vogue of placing faith in "abstract religion." Joining Paul Tillich, Hannah Arendt, and Jacques Maritain in the *Partisan Review*'s 1950 discussion of "Religion and the Intellectuals," he spoke out as an "amateur" theologian, skeptical of the vulgar moralism of postwar religion-in-general. Like the dead in Dante's *Comedy*, Tate said, authentic religion must possess flesh and bone: the creed, rite, and authority of "a definite religion."[112]

Quaestiones Disputatae

Writing Donald Davidson soon after his baptism, Tate revealed the full extent of this important side of his religious sensibilities. Instead of explaining his recent conversion, he simply related accounts of enjoyable visits to St. John's Abbey in Minnesota, including a note on his discovery of the "complete skeleton" of Saint Peregrinus, the *puer* martyr of the second century. "As you know," Tate instructed his agnostic friend, "we are under no obligation of faith to believe that these bones are Peregrin's, but it is pleasant to be engaged by the perspective opened up by the possibility."[113]

Perhaps what Tate actually saw when he peered into the glass of the Benedictine reliquary was the peculiar genius of his newly chosen religion to launch the loftiest metaphysical quest from the lowliest matter of ordinary reality. Thomas Aquinas had declared that "we can name God only from creatures," and the German theologian Karl Adam had proclaimed art's reverence for nature and for the body a "native" feature of the Catholic theological tradition.[114] That basic insight into the sacramental character of material and temporal creation served as the organizing principle for Tate's developing religious criticism. In the calculus of his unique religious experience, it was the bones of Peregrin—or rather the necessity of the religious imagination to transport ancient bones from European crypts to the American Middle West—that transformed Tate's complaint against "the synthesis of pure abstraction" into a prophetic program of religious criticism.[115] For Tate, it meant the difference between "mere" Christianity and the fullness of Christian faith.

That aspect of Tate's religious criticism was the product of the intersection of his artistic sentiments with his creative appropriation of contemporary Neo-Thomism. As John Dunaway has suggested, Tate came to the Catholic Church by an intellectual path similar to that traveled by the model twentieth-century convert Maritain.[116] Disenchanted with the reigning scientific naturalism of the Sorbonne, the young Maritain had discovered in Aquinas' thought a metaphysical system capable of healing the divided modern mind through its synthesis of the natural and the supernatural. Tate, too, found Thomism a compelling testimony to the unity of truth and experience, an inviting alternative to the cold positivism of the academy. In contrast to Maritain's highly philosophical experience, however, Tate's conversion was greatly determined by the distinctive discipline of his aesthetic vision. As he described it a decade after the event, the instincts that drove him from the abstraction of modernity also directed him into the least abstract form of Christianity available at the time. "My writings," he confessed, "have influenced my religious beliefs." Once convinced that the same impulse requiring the literary imagination to seek an "incarnation of reality" in language constituted the heart of the Catholic religious imagination—especially its foundational intuition regarding the possibility of God's "embodiment"—Tate drew upon the authority of Catholic thought to expand his critique of modernity's abstraction into a full-scale review of gnostic influences in modern society.[117]

Ironically, the first place the Catholic critic Tate detected heretical tendencies was within the Catholic Church itself. James Hitchcock has defined the "Gnostic failure of imagination" as the incapacity to recognize the imperfect vehicles of human and historical reality as means for the revelation of divine transcendence.[118] That failure was precisely the defect Tate discovered in the literature produced and consumed by his fellow American Catholics. As a new convert, demonstrating something of the legendary zeal and arrogance of that state, Tate immediately entered the contemporary debate concerning the moral obligations of art and the issue of clerical censorship. Convinced that he had found evidence of the gnostic quest for perfection and purity within America's Catholic literary establishment, he published an open letter in the *New York Times*, challenging the critical competence of New York's outspoken Cardinal Francis Spellman. Questioning Spellman's condemnation of the recently released Italian film, "The Miracle," Tate suggested that the drive on the part of some Catholics to suppress the controversial motion picture in the United States pointed to "a latent heresy within the church."[119] Two years later, in reaction to the sentimental piety of the American Catholic novel, especially Spellman's newly published book, *The Foundling*, Tate stressed the practical heresy of the ostensibly orthodox writer. Instead of a vigorous witness to the universality of original sin, which even the nascent country music industry of his native region could deliver as a bedrock conviction, America's mediocre Catholic literature conveyed to Tate only cultural captivity to "a secular dispensation of which the perfectibility of man has been the easy dogma."[120] In what was originally a talk addressed to a university Newman Club audience, Tate echoed the famous nineteenth-century convert's contention that a "sinless Literature of sinful man" is a contradiction.[121] For Tate, the responsibility of the truly orthodox Catholic writer was not to protect delicate Christian sensibilities from the harsh realities of worldly existence but "to portray the human experience as it is, whether he likes it or not."[122]

In 1958, Tate summed up these criticisms in his Christian Culture address at Ontario's Assumption University. On the subject of the pitiful lack of talent or excellence in Spellman's literary oeuvre, Tate said:

> The Catholic sacramental life offers us one kind of discipline, but it is not the literary discipline. The power to see this difference...[is] a subtle cooperation of the intellectual and the moral which is generally the mark of the civilized mind....Until it is possible for the Catholic critic, clerical as well as lay, to denounce inferior secular writing by the clergy, even if the clergy happens to

be represented by a Cardinal, we shall not have taken the first step towards the creation of a high Catholic culture.

On the more serious question of censorship, Tate cast the Legion of Decency's eagerness to crusade against female nudity in films, while ignoring the broader "vulgarity of the Hollywood view of life," as "something like Puritanism or even Jansenism and Manicheanism [sic]—one heresy combatting another." Citing Newman's *Idea of a University* on the imperial intellect's virtue of discrimination, Tate linked the issue to the larger hope for a genuine Catholic Revival:

> Not all Cardinals can be Newmans, nor all laymen imperial intellects. But I think it is not too much to expect, in the not too distant future, the reappearance of a Catholic intelligence which flourished in the three centuries from about the year 1100. If it does not reappear, the Church will nevertheless keep open the channels of salvation, even though we complacently populate Heaven with barbarians.[123]

"With the Body of This World"

At the heart of Tate's holy war for orthodoxy, the key doctrine that informed his critique of the church's capitulation to popular heresy was Maritain's free interpretation of the Thomistic notion of connaturality. Originally, Aquinas had observed a certain analogical affinity between the conditions of nature and the way human minds learn truths beyond nature. Maritain developed that idea, translating it into a principle of "creative intuition in art and poetry," not unlike what Jesuit theologian Bernard Lonergan would call "incarnate meaning" or the dynamic form of knowledge available through aesthetic experience.[124] Like many literary friends of Catholicism around mid-century, Tate learned his Thomism from Maritain without any imposition of doctrinaire scruples regarding thirteenth-century authorial intentions. Uninterested in its technical scholastic meaning, he used the term "connaturality" as something of an authoritative code word for "analogical thinking," the dominant principle, according to Maritain, in all modern Thomisms. For Tate, it became the basic insight nurturing his views of church and culture.[125]

Tate's intellectual debt to Maritain was most clearly evidenced by the pair of lectures he delivered at Boston College in 1951. In these works, he employed Maritain's Thomistic categories to define the dilemma constituting modern existence as the "Cartesian split" wrenching the self from the world. Contrasting the literary visions of Dante and the nineteenth-century American writer Edgar Allan Poe, "The Symbolic Imagination" and "The Angelic Imagination" represented for Tate not only alternative approaches to the creative intellect but competing views of the meaning and purpose of culture as well. Using Maritain's famous neologism, Tate rendered Poe's "angelism"—his gnostic contempt for the restrictions placed upon the imagination by physical existence—as a symptom of the faulty anthropology subverting modern Western culture. By contrast, he recommended the medieval Dante as the prime representative of the self-understanding at the basis of the "great culture" nourished by the life of the Catholic Church. Like Protestant "realist" Reinhold Niebuhr, Tate believed that the fate of the West turned in large part on its ability to recover the sober understanding of human nature articulated in orthodox Christian tradition. He linked the Catholic writer's personal loss of "the gift for concrete experience" to the church's historic loss of a culture whose institutions recognized both the divine origins and fallen conditions of all its human constituents. Consequently, when he exhorted the modern poet "to do his work with the body of this world, whatever that body may look like to him," Tate was not proposing merely an application of Thomistic epistemological theory to literary exegesis. Rather, conforming to the Christ-above-culture model of H. Richard Niebuhr's synthetic type, he was urging a strategic response to the cultural consequences of mass heresy.[126]

In its review of the Boston College Candlemas Lectures, the Catholic journal *Thought* found in Tate "a well-knit man capable of imparting a surprising unity of vision."[127] In his subsequent international speaking engagements, Tate broadened this critical unity of vision in order to include analysis of contemporary global issues, thereby establishing his place in the intellectual milieu that Patrick Carey has described as "Cold War Catholicism."[128] Alarmed by the growth of totalitarian societies on both sides of the Iron Curtain, Tate applied his critique of modern gnosticism to the varieties of secular collectivism that he saw threatening public life and individual liberties around the world. Speaking along with Etienne Gilson, Martin D'Arcy, and Jean Daniélou at the 1954 Congress for Peace and Christian Civilization in Florence, he interpreted the postwar danger of totalitarianism as the product of a gnostic secularism disjoining human experience from the moral and physical restraints of the authentic humanity revealed in the Christian tradition. Reflecting on the significance of the international conference, Tate wrote:

> It is of the utmost importance, in a period of history which marks the collapse of the Renaissance doctrine of the self-sufficiency of

Man, that Christians from all over the world should meet to aknowledge [sic] the power of supernatural guidance in secular affairs....Culture is that particular point in the secular experience at which revelation makes its first impact.[129]

In his official Congress address, "Christ and the Unicorn," Tate decried what he took to be the key factor responsible for both the regimented bureaucratic societies of the West and the communist dictatorships of the Eastern Bloc: the uncritical acceptance of the Enlightenment's heresy of the "omnipotence of reason" and its twin, the modern heresy of the "omnicompetent state." Anxious to unmask both the fictions of the communist world and the modernist fantasies of a self-congratulatory West, Tate attempted to demonstrate how both social heresies failed to reckon with the biblical vision of the relationship between the divine and the human. Bolstering his conclusions with quotations from Distributist historian Douglas Jerrold, he predicted the rise of "a complete Gnostic society," should the West abandon its fundamentally religious insights into the human condition. "One need not be a theologian," he observed, "to see that the two cooperating heresies represent a total rejection of the Incarnation."[130] Along with Maritain and Dawson, Tate maintained that any hope for an authentically democratic future in national or international affairs necessitated the acceptance of a genuinely Christian humanism. Like Chesterton, who identified the dogma of the incarnate Logos as the idea "central in our civilisation,"[131] he placed the Christological mystery at the heart of his analysis of culture. Without that controlling idea, he said, every quest for the perfect society yields only another "perishable god" for the scrap heap of the world's worthless idols: "I have come to the view that no society is worth 'saving' *as such*: what we must save is the truth of God and Man, and the right society follows."[132]

"A Catholic Matthew Arnold"

In his discussion of Tate's prophetic role as religious critic, Gale Carrithers has accurately observed that the stock stereotypes of anti-modern apostate and new American Saint Paul do not adequately describe Tate's place in modern intellectual history. Indeed, Tate was neither the untimely-born scholastic clerk that Lewis P. Simpson once imagined, nor even the "quasi-Hebraic" prophet, engaged in modern iconoclasm, that Carrithers himself has pictured.[133] Rather, the image that best captures Tate's sense of prophetic mission is one gleaned from his own imagination. Soon after his baptism, as he lamented the sad state of Catholic intellectual life in America—what he derisively called the "Know-Nothingism of Catholic 'intellectuals' in this country"[134]—Tate declared that what his new community desperately needed was a "Catholic Matthew Arnold"—a public intellectual of taste and discernment to reflect upon and judge current affairs.[135] Like the magisterial Victorian critic, Tate understood the "present function of criticism" to be a defense of the forms of culture in "the dark ages of our present enlightenment."[136] Just as Arnold sought to secure a ghetto of civility against the assaults of a new barbarian civilization, Tate attempted to protect the foundational insights of classical Christianity from the cultural erosion threatening vital Western institutions. Instead of anarchy, which bothered Arnold, what Tate feared was the construction of a new religion to express the unlimited pieties of an emerging culture innocent of the constraints placed upon humans in nature and history. For Tate, the new gnosticism was not so much the decline of reverenced standards—though it certainly included that—as the frank and un-Christian denial of the human situation in physical body and body politic.

Thomas Altizer has recently connected the loss of transcendence in modernist experience to the triumph of the "plain style" in American speech and writing, a pattern of discourse "stripped not only of rhetorical embellishment, but more deeply of human and historical tradition."[137] Similarly, Tate rendered the disappearance of the analogical imagination, linking the concrete realm of natural phenomenon and human convention to the inner life of the mind, as a graphic sign of the West's disturbing betrayal of its intellectual patrimony. Far from a mere literary event, the "vaporization of religion" that his young literary friend, Flannery O'Connor, traced from Emerson's transparent eyeball to the blank stare of her own Hazel Motes served for Tate as a ghostly token of the insidious heresies menacing the Western world. Contrary to its academic stereotype, Tate's New Criticism drew him from the classroom into the Catholic Revival's struggle for the soul of modernity. According to him, the critic had significant responsibilities that were "more than literary," social duties, possessing connaturality with aesthetic trusts, that entailed reacquainting the disembodied modern imagination with the "concrete forms" necessary for meaningful social and religious existence.[138] Concerned about modern Christianity's ability to withstand its ancient gnostic foe, Tate entered the service of the church ready to do his part, as Leo prescribed, "for the defense and beauty of the Catholic faith, for the good of society, and for the advantage of all the sciences."

5 | Traveler Lost in a Forest

Converted men as a class are indistinguishable from natural men.
—William James[1]

Modern converts in every country have to be like birds escaped from cages; Catholics to the manor born may be apostolic like you or sceptics like me, but we feel at home in any case and don't ride hobbies.
—Santayana to Cyril Clemens[2]

In the prime years of his Catholic experience, Allen Tate articulated a vision of church and culture that questioned a set of assumptions regarding orthodoxy that had attained currency in the American Catholic community. In the last years of his career, by contrast, his criticism took a more personal turn. To some extent, he assumed the persona of the lonely prophet crying in the wilderness of modernity, the voice of the "dispossessed and forlorn orthodoxy" that Santayana had pinned on Eliot. At the same time, however, Tate was forced to face the cruel fact that self-appointed champions of orthodoxy can only rarely escape the snares of heresy in a world shaped by the heretical impulse itself. In fact, as the dramatic moment of his conversion drifted into the past, it became apparent to even the most sympathetic observers that Tate himself was not immune from the tendencies of what he called the "angelic" imagination. Aware of the well-documented tradition of modern self-deception, Tate pointed to places in his own thought where the forces of "Gnostic despair and Gnostic intellectual pride" prevailed over the prudent vision of Christian humanism.[3] As Daniel Joseph Singal has suggested, a deep ambivalence regarding the requisite commitments of communal authority haunted each stage of Tate's career—even his search for tradition and his acceptance of the Catholic religion, what he thought would be the antidote to modern heresy.[4] Tate himself never denied that. His private letters from the last decades of his life make it clear that he questioned his ability to live up to the rigorous standards of his own Christian criticism. From his perspective, however, the unique vocation of the modern Christian critic lay precisely in the awareness of the deep-seated properties of "Gnostic arrogance" and "Augustinian humility" in the modern soul—that strange mixture of nihilism and naïveté raised in the shadow of the mushroom cloud. That psychological constitution, Tate believed, qualified the modern writer to function as something of a wounded healer, a reliable witness to the true state of the modern world and its need for redemption. Given the pervasive heresies of the age, he said, the prophetic critic must "warn us...to come out of our Gnostic dream of perfection into the actual world, where human reality is in the commitment to the limited human condition, which allows us only the irony of imperfect love."[5]

A photograph of Tate, taken in 1976 on the occasion of an award ceremony celebrating his literary achievement, graphically reveals to what extent his Catholic experience came to embody such limitations and ironies.[6] The picture, shot in the library of Aquinas College in Nashville, Tennessee, shows the seventy-seven-year-old critic surrounded by a group of admirers, including two Catholic sisters in Dominican habit. An unflattering portrait, it looks as if the photographer caught the ailing writer at an awkward moment. Unlike his beaming companions, Tate, dressed in old-fashioned business suit with handkerchief in breast pocket, looks haggard and uncomfortable. Eyes downcast, body bent forward, left hand gripping his chair, the guest of honor, afflicted by emphysema and ulcers, seems oddly out of place at his own reception. Despite his ironclad reputation for impeccable manners, he appears unimpressed by the recognition bestowed upon him by the college. The frail subject of the photograph betrays the look of a man receiving honor too late and from the hands of strangers.

The Catholic Church of the American bicentennial year was not the same church that Tate had worked so hard to enter decades earlier. The church that would bury him within three years possessed only a vague family resemblance to the institution that had first enchanted him half a century before. Tate entered the Roman Catholic Church at a major turning point in its modern experience. By the time he received its seventh sacrament, it had passed through an ordeal matchless in modern Christian history. Like the last of a people who had sailed to a far country, Tate witnessed not only the end of his race but the change of tide that wiped from shore all signs of their legendary migration. As fellow Revival convert Julian Green had realized that "only from the outside do conversions appear to simplify life's problems,"[7] Tate came to see that conversion itself represented a significant problem.

"The Trials of a Mind"

Writing to a friend in 1958, Flannery O'Connor said that "all good stories are about conversion." Instinctively, she knew that the nature of narrative discourse itself demanded the careful tracing of a character's mental and moral transformation as it led over time to a crucial moment of decision. Turning then to the specific subject of religious conversion, she added: "If it is the Church he's converted to, the Church remains stable and he has to change."[8] By definition, she assumed, a conversion to Catholic Christianity dictated a special kind of narrative. The real drama of religious conversion happened before the climactic surrender to authority or the final act of a profession of faith. After that, conversion ceased and the challenges of ordinary fidelity commenced. Given this paradigm, conversion proceeded according to its own discursive logic, moving in steady stages or in fits and starts toward some sort of spiritually satisfying culmination. "Then comes the mellowing time," as Katherine Bregy observed, "the adjustment and readjustment of ideas, the rounding of sharp corners, the gradual *ceasing to be a convert*."[9] The standard archetypes and dynamics of conversion, governed by traditional conventions, focused on the agonizing quest for unshakable faith or the irrepressible search for a changeless church. Life after conversion, admittedly, did not stir the imagination. Who, after all, had ever read much beyond Book VIII of Augustine's *Confessions*?

In their reflections on the mystery of conversion, what O'Connor and Bregy failed to imagine was a conversion story in which even the church remained in constant motion. For them, as well as for Catholics of several generations, it was virtually impossible to conceive of a Catholic conversion that could require of the subject the unique ability to negotiate not only the crisis of personal *metanoia* but also a bewildering pattern of continual change in a spiritual landscape of constantly shifting landmarks.

When the Catholic Church entered the period of its greatest trial since the sixteenth century, such a pattern became the normative narrative for modern Catholic conversion. Conversion to Catholicism became less a matter of supreme surrender initiating ultimate peace and more a mode of survival in a community marked by perpetual reformation. One could even say that the church as a whole experienced the refining fire of conversion. In the deceptive serenity of the Eisenhower years, the American Catholic Church approached such a "revolutionary moment" (to use James Hennesey's apt phrase)[10] when cradle Catholics would act like converts and converts feel like strangers.

Ushering in a period of long overdue self-examination and unparalleled moral testing, the mid-century transformation of Catholicism overturned all previous notions of Catholic piety and conversion. Together, Catholics of all kinds discovered what one of Robert Penn Warren's characters called "the awful responsibility of Time."[11]

An examination of earlier conversion literature confirms that such was not always the case. From individual narratives to the anthologies recording various *Roads to Rome*,[12] every Catholic Revival conversion story represented a variation on a universally recognizable plot line. A modern form of martyrdom, as Belloc put it, conversion to Catholicism functioned as a witness to the unchangeable truth of Catholic belief in a world of mutable half-truths. Testifying to what Evelyn Waugh called the "eternal character" of the Catholic faith,[13] Chesterton said, "The Catholic Church is the only thing which saves a man from the degrading slavery of being a child of his age."[14]

Conversion narratives from the nineteenth-century Catholic Revival demonstrate the implications of these widespread convictions. One of the more startling statements in Newman's *Apologia*, for example, occurs in the context of his reflections on the steady state of his intellectual life after his acceptance of Catholicism in 1845. Writing about the position of his mind since that year, Newman said:

> From the time that I became a Catholic, of course, I have no further history of my religious opinions to narrate....I have had no changes to record, and have had no anxiety of heart whatever. I have been in perfect peace and contentment. I never have had one doubt.[15]

Even without the surprising "of course," signaling the author's status as master stylist of polite Victorian prose, the claim is nothing short of remarkable. It stands in elegant contrast to modernity's assumptions regarding the proper course of intellectual life. For Newman, despite all his noble talk of development and change, stability and certainty were the qualities that defined the goal of conversion and brought intellectual history to its ordained end. Around the same time, on the other side of the Atlantic, in the thick of America's Oxford Movement, another former member of the Anglican communion wrote of the curious relation between intellectual life and religious conversion. L. Sullivan Ives, the Protestant Episcopal bishop of North Carolina who quit the *via media* for the Roman Church, wrote a defense of his spiritual defection that fed the suspicions of Nativist critics who associated Catholicism with intellectual stagnation. Writing in 1854, he rehearsed the narrative of his conversion in *The Trials of a Mind in its Progress to Catholicism*. Significantly, like Newman, he did not find it necessary to record for posterity the trials that his mind had had to endure after its progression to Catholicism. For him, conversion afforded only "new and unutterable joy."[16]

For these writers and for scores of others associated with the twentieth-century Catholic Revival, conversion meant what it did for the premier student of religious experience, William James: the process "by which a self hitherto divided, and consciously wrong inferior and unhappy, becomes unified and consciously right, superior and happy."[17] Conversion, it was believed, brought the restless spiritual pilgrim out of aimless wilderness wanderings into near perfect sabbath repose. Even Merton's *Seven Storey Mountain*, perhaps the last example of the classic narrative tradition, runs out of dramatic steam when the author for the final time rings Gethsemani's cloister bell and enters the church's realm of timeless tranquility.

Compared to other converts of the Catholic Revival, Allen Tate was not so lucky. Like Charles Reding in Newman's *Loss and Gain* (1886), he equated the Catholic religion with a reliable "system" that would provide the critical perspective for the chaotic world of modern thought to connect "fact with fact, truth with truth."[18] What Tate did not count on, however, was the rapid unraveling of that system in the post-conversion years of his Catholic experience. In the novel, young Reding, Newman's fictional alter ego, lives in a time of confusion when "viewy" men have recourse to no trustworthy authority for their many and ambitious opinions. With its dogmatic creed, its venerable rite, and its apostolic hierarchy, Roman Catholicism enters Reding's world as a complete system of objective certitude free from the vicissitudes of religion based on speculation and private judgment. He abandons the Anglican faith of his family and Oxford training precisely at the time when this Catholic system is undergoing an intense process of consolidation.

Tate, too, knew the appeal of the Catholic system. The ethos of preconciliar Catholicism, dedicated to the best in the Western intellectual tradition and protecting it with the hedge of Neo-Thomistic efforts in the arts and sciences, seemed to him the only acceptable cultural climate for authentic faith. In contrast to the fictional Reding, however, Tate discovered the very real and uncertain nature of twentieth-century religious experience. In near textbook fashion, his conversion entailed the painful encounter with what sociologist Peter Berger has called "the problem of ecclesial belonging."[19] As Richard Foster observed in 1962, "the place where [Tate] has chosen to lay his final allegiance has itself become the origin of a new creative process."[20]

"A Lonely Way"

As he attempted to pursue his vocation in the church, Tate felt the first tremors of what Philip Gleason has called the "spiritual earthquake" of mid-century Catholic history.[21] Contrary to the high expectations of many leaders in the Catholic community, Tate's efforts to establish himself as America's "Catholic Matthew Arnold" produced only shaky results, and his initiatives as a Catholic religious critic yielded few tangible successes. Despite his international prominence as a Catholic man of letters and the many invitations from Catholic quarters requesting lectures and publications, Tate never gained a meaningful position of leadership in the Catholic Revival movement. In fact, the Revival itself, already showing signs of atrophy by the 1950s, seemed to frustrate the distinguished convert's Catholic ambitions. Harbingers of troubles to come, several developments contributed to this state of affairs.

Initially, Tate was hesitant to embrace more than the general values of the Catholic Revival. Nagging doubts regarding the Revival's intellectual integrity still festered in Tate's mind. Always a problem for the church, as Lawrence Cunningham has observed,[22] the vision of Christian humanism required public dedication to the values of the gospel and unwavering allegiance to the highest standards of secular culture. In Tate's case, the precarious balance of commitments in the humanist's vocation sabotaged his ability to act with confidence in the community of Catholic Revival proponents. Publicly bemoaning the inferior state of American Catholic literature, Tate was eager to launch a genuinely Catholic Renaissance governed by the rigorous literary standards of high modernism. His stubborn aesthetic scruples, however, prevented him from collaborating effectively with the Catholic leaders most inclined to welcome his professional assistance. Though attracted by the myth of the Catholic Revival, Tate never became an active participant in the movement's main organizations. He persistently found the institutions of the American Revival flawed. To Francis X. Connolly of the Catholic Poetry Society, he wrote:

> I cannot see in American Catholicism more than a remnant of the great [Catholic] tradition....The reviews of my books by Catholic writers or by the Catholic press in England and France have been the most enlightening intellectually that I have had; the reviews by American Catholics have been grossly ignorant, narrowly sectarian, and merely moralistic and censorious. There is overwhelming evidence that American Catholicism has lost the critical and artistic phase of its tradition.[23]

Similarly, he explained his objections to *A. D.*'s editor, Thomas Francis Ritt:

> I take it that the Kingdom of God will not consent to be served with mediocrity from the republic of letters....We shall not create a great Catholic literary culture in this country by abusing the great non-Catholic literary culture of our immediate past. It seems to me that our task is to learn from it and at least to equal it.[24]

For Tate, the institutions of the Catholic Revival revealed the embarrassing gap between the movement's single-minded rhetoric and its protean achievements. Many in the movement's leadership actually agreed with his criticism of Catholicism's mixed record in cultural affairs. In *America*, for example, Vincent Blehl maintained that the Catholic writer

> must become immersed in two traditions. As artist or critic he must master on the one hand the techniques of his craft and the English and American literary tradition, and on the other, he must acquire a more profound awareness of his Catholic heritage than many Catholic artists or critics have heretofore possessed.[25]

Despite such currents of self-criticism within the Revival, Tate remained ambivalent about potential alliances with Catholic educators and publishers. Referring once to the Jesuit scholar Gustave Weigel, he said, "If there were more [priests] like him there would be a real Catholic renascence."[26]

At those points where he did attempt to enter the work of the Catholic Revival, Tate habitually ran into other discouraging roadblocks. He found little support in Revival circles for initiating projects of his own. His endeavor to enlist likely participants in his "Conversations at Newburgh" project, for example, proved especially disappointing. Though Walter Ong and other Catholic intellectuals responded with polite encouragement to his vision of a Catholic community of letters on Dorothy Day's New York farm, only a few devoted their energies to the practical task of organizing the school. What could have been the Bread Loaf School of American Catholic writing entered the history of American literature stillborn. Strapped by academic or ecclesiastical duties, many potential supporters could not afford to invest scarce resources in such a risky venture. Others, less willing to endorse the unconventional proposal, harbored doubts about the wisdom of the idea itself. William Lynch, for example, candidly resisted the project for fear of being associated with the eccentricities of the countercultural Catholic Worker crowd.[27]

Another problem complicating Tate's relationship with the Revival revolved around the issue of public recognition. Despite his harsh criticism of Catholic literature's accomplishments, Tate apparently felt neglected by the Revival's literary establishment. Like Harry Sylvester, he knew first-hand the classic "problems of the Catholic writer."[28] As Richard Hofstadter put it, the native anti-intellectual ethos of American Catholicism ensured that Catholic writers would "tend to be recognized belatedly by their co-religionists, when they are recognized at all."[29] Venting his emotions in a letter to Caroline Gordon, Tate grumbled about the slim coverage of his career in Catholic journals like *Thought* and *Renascence*. In addition, his jealousies were aroused by the lavish attention that Catholics devoted to the work of the younger Robert Lowell, even after Lowell's rejection of Catholicism in favor of the Episcopal Church. "What puts these people off," Tate told Gordon, "is that we take Catholicism seriously as writers, and it is too tough for them. So we must go a lonely way so far as the Church is concerned."[30]

"A Person Without a Vocation"

In the late 1950s, Tate discovered his way in the Catholic Church to be far lonelier than he had ever expected. While the internal dynamics of the Revival movement fed his apprehension about his role in the church, troublesome developments in his personal life contributed to what was becoming the subversion of his Catholic aspirations. Tremors in his family life severely crippled his relationship with the Revival movement and the larger Catholic community. Previously divorced and remarried in 1946, the Tates had always known the trials of a rocky marriage. Even during the early years of their common life as new Catholic converts, the couple had struggled to overcome the violent clash of their temperaments, tenacious financial problems, the burdens of alcoholism, and nasty rumors of extramarital affairs. Then, in 1955, after Tate's academic year alone in Europe, he and Gordon separated for a second time. Just as *Thought* issued church historian John Tracy Ellis' now famous challenge to foster the general intellectual life of American Catholicism, Tate's future as a Catholic intellectual seemed particularly uncertain.

During this period, Tate's letters to Gordon revealed the intensity of his chronic "spiritual unease"—a crisis of spirit aggravated by fears of alcohol abuse and unnamed demons exorcised only by "holding on to a rosary all night." Read as a body, the letters unfold the drama of a soul in desperate search for meaning. They tell of extensive dream analysis in Rome with a Jungian clinician and of additional psychotherapy with a Catholic psychiatrist after Tate's return to America. They also show to what extent Tate set his personal reflections in the context of his on-going spiritual reading. Discussions of emotional trials, counseling sessions, and joint financial challenges—the standard fare of the discourse of American divorce—are linked to exegesis of Maritain on marriage, D'Arcy on knowledge and love, Gilson on mystical theology, Carl Jung on the Trinity, and even parallels between the exotic texts of the Upanishads and the gospels. For one thing, the correspondence clearly demonstrates how Tate increasingly attempted to find a pragmatic answer to his spiritual dilemma in the fusion of classic Catholic devotion with current trends in psychology. Approaching "a new phase for which I haven't yet found the right language, except perhaps on the theological level," he looked for help in the creative synthesis of depth psychology and contemporary theology—what he considered the modern equivalent of Aquinas' reconciliation of Aristotle with Christian revelation.[31] More importantly, the letters to Gordon dispel for the objective reader all doubts regarding the personal significance of Tate's desire to establish a home in the world of Catholic myth and meaning. His worries about their failed marriage and, later, the possibility of an annulment habitually turned to the question of his identity as a "complete" Catholic, especially "the intermittent belief that I am abandoned by God." Calling their troubles "an anticipation of Purgatory," he regularly framed his interpretation of their situation in the language of the mystic's purgative way. John of the Cross, he suggested, was the spiritual director for such people on the margins of the church's grace. "We can learn from him," he said, "even if we can never get quite beyond the Dark Night of Sense. Isn't that about the limit of the spiritual achievement for people *in* the world?"[32]

By 1959, the year of the Tates' second divorce and his subsequent remarriage to the poet Isabella Gardner, Tate, according to his own frank analysis, was fast becoming a "person without a vocation" in the Catholic Church. Not only was he a layman distant from the special graces of the religious life; he was also a prominent Catholic convert straining the limits of the church's hospitality. By all charitable standards of measure, his status as a public Catholic intellectual was in severe jeopardy. Nevertheless, his self-understanding as a Catholic remained surprisingly intact. Barred from full participation in the sacramental life of the church, he still assisted at the liturgy, "perforce at a distance." He even insisted that he continued to exercise his intellectual apostolate—"in my way, and perhaps more effectively than I did before I was out of Communion."[33] It was a sense of honor, he said, that kept him a Catholic without the church, committed as ever to the formal dogmas of the tradition yet resentful of the church's "legalistic" canon law.[34] Though Catholic speaking invitations dropped off for fear of scandal and former Catholic colleagues increasingly found themselves in the awkward position of having to speculate on the canonical validity of his marriage, not all members of the Catholic intellectual community forgot the one who was to be their century's Newman. William Lynch wrote to reassure the "paradoxical" pilgrim: "That you cannot go to the Sacraments does not mean you are cut off from the total life of the Church....I do not at all give you up and your great vocation in God's service."[35]

"Slaying of the Fathers"

Such optimistic sentiments seriously miscalculated the signs of the times. Compounding Tate's problems, public and private, was the radically declining force of the Catholic Revival itself. By the 1950s, faithful participants in the Revival noticed that the movement had begun to wane. As Arnold Sparr has made clear, the mainstreaming tendencies of postwar American Catholicism led proponents of the Revival to question the wisdom of efforts to build a distinctively Catholic alternative culture.[36] Even members of the Catholic Renascence Society were convinced to abandon the quest for a uniquely Catholic literature in favor of more ecumenical ambitions. Ironically, the New Criticism of Tate and colleagues had much to do with the Society's decision. While recognizing that New Criticism represented "the revival of a principle that belongs to our heritage and may be found in St. Thomas," John Pick, editor of *Renascence* magazine, realized that the future of Catholic letters depended solely on the acceptance of universal literary standards, not the singular possession of religious truth. "When we manage to concentrate on the work of art itself," he editorialized, "then and only then will our criticism win the respect of intelligent readers—whether they be Catholics or not."[37] Catholic exceptionalism, it seemed, stood in the way of genuine literary criticism.

In other intellectual circles, the Revival's countercultural world view that Tate had found so inspiring was now threatened by competing values and ideologies. Catholic medievalism and antimodernism fell victim to a generous re-evaluation of modernity's promise, just as Catholic agrarianism, once the prophetic vogue, seemed embarrassingly anachronistic to Catholics finding a niche in the environment of the postwar economy.[38] New confidence in notions of democratic individualism and free enterprise replaced old doubts about the Enlightenment and its political and economic children. Likewise, theological dissatisfaction with the hegemony of neo-scholastic philosophy started to erode the accepted intellectual framework of the church. New efforts in the discipline of historical theology led a growing number of scholars to question the legitimacy of elevating one period of Christian thought to a normative status above the plurality of traditions in the church's intellectual canon. Driven by a spirit of *ressourcement*, they expressed fresh interest in the biblical and patristic sources of Christian thought. The *nouvelle theologie* of a young theological generation destined to triumph among the clerical *periti* at Vatican II gradually eclipsed the reigning Neo-Thomism in the halls of Catholic academia. The impact of the mounting ecumenical movement on Catholic theology also encouraged the trend toward theological re-evaluation. Making the emphasis on Catholic distinctives intellectually unfashionable, ecumenism undermined the dynamics behind the Revival's spirit of Catholic triumphalism and its astonishing record of conversions.

In the broader Catholic community, the processes of change in religious life, set in motion by the destabilizing influence of World War II, effectively shook the social context for preconciliar Catholic ritual, belief, and identity. The war itself, seen as the triumph of liberal democracy over all rival forces, discredited any lingering desire among Catholics to defend Pius IX's old condemnation of progress, liberalism, and modern civilization. The Allied victory over the neo-paganism of the Nazis and the theocratic nationalism of the Japanese empire seemed to justify the kind of secular democratic culture created by modernity. After the war, European rates of church attendance dropped off severely, and ecclesiastical observers feared a wave of post-Christian secularism sweeping over the continent. At the same time, in America, what sociologist Robert Wuthnow has called a "restructuring" of denominational life began to cut away at commonly held assumptions about Catholic uniqueness.[39] Upwardly mobile Catholics sought to free themselves from the cultural constraints of the ethnic Catholic ghetto, while young Catholic veterans entering universities on the G. I. Bill tried to slough off the emblems of their parochial education. The forces that would fuel John F. Kennedy's bid for the White House inaugurated a new relationship between Catholicism and secular American culture. The rising fortunes of a Catholic community anxious to form lasting ties with capitalist prosperity and academic respectability undermined the continued existence of a style of religion associated with the tribal subcultures of "hyphenated" citizens. Moreover, mass defections from religious orders and the priest-hood, beginning even before the close of the Second Vatican Council, dramatically altered the church's extensive womb-to-tomb institutional life.

In addition to these developments, the educated Catholic public, once the dependable audience for Revival literature disseminated by Sheed and Ward, began to turn to new sources of information and authority. The young intellectuals of the 1950s known as "*Commonweal* Catholics", sought their inspiration without regard to sectarian scruples or ecclesiastical affiliation. Meanwhile, the leading writers of the Revival slipped from their position of previously unquestioned prestige. Chesterton had died in 1936 leaving no heir to his post as intellectual propagandist for the Revival, while Belloc, who did not live beyond 1953, produced no work of significant merit after the Depression years. Other Revival figures, such as Christopher Dawson and Maritain, sur-vived long enough to witness the crash of their intellectual stock in the ideological reversals of the 1960s.

For its part, Vatican II, especially as interpreted by the religious press and rank-and-file Catholics, laid out a startlingly new way of being Catholic. From the perspective of many observers, the Second Vatican Council was a revolution. As John O'Malley has stated, "Never before in the history of Catholicism have so many and such sudden changes been legislated and implemented which immediately touched the lives of the faithful, and never before had such a radical adjustment of viewpoint been required of them."[40] The Council's updating of liturgical practice and church administration contributed to new perceptions of the rela-tivity of religious obligations and the limits of ecclesiastical authority. Proponents of reform measures viewed the Council's call for *aggiorna-mento* as simply a first step toward extensive institutional change. A new crop of influential leaders issued mandates for the modernization of basic dogmas, the democratization of church structures, the liberaliza-tion of canon law, and the "de-Romanization" of Catholicism itself.[41] They greeted the Council as "not an end but a beginning."[42] German theologian Karl Rahner, for example, interpreted the Council in world-historical terms, calling it an event unique in Christian history that promised a new age of global spiritual renewal.[43] Even before it was well under way, insiders hailed the Council as "a new Pentecost," and hope-ful non-Catholic observers called it a "catalyst for change."[44]

By contrast, critics of progressive understandings of the Council regarded postconciliar ventures in reform as unwarranted accommoda-tions to the worst aspects of modernity. Limiting the spirit of the Council to the letter of the conciliar documents, they derided new departures in liturgy, architecture, music, and theology as signs of the foolish rejection of classical Christianity's cultural treasure. They branded the fervor of postconciliarism as the insanity of people destroying what it would take them centuries to recreate. In 1964, for instance, the pensive progressive Thomas Merton worried "that in the reforms and renovation that are now under way there may be no end of hasty, ill-considered and sweeping changes in which a lot that is profoundly significant and alive will be discarded thoughtlessly."[45] Other critics, fixated especially on the dramatic course of liturgical change, shuddered at what they considered a reckless iconoclasm bordering on vandalism. Just as a class of social critics had blamed modernity for the quality of flatness in modern industrial society, critics of the postconciliar church indicted popular understandings of the Council with the systematic impoverishment of Catholic life.

Disaffected leaders, feeling a deep sense of betrayal, expressed apprehension concerning the Catholic Church's future. The popular television personality, Bishop Fulton Sheen, an American participant in the Council, thought that the Council's reputation had been hijacked by forces of secularism. He pointed to the cruel irony of a church experiencing a "decline of spirituality" at the very moment when it should have enjoyed an unprecedented resurgence of piety.[46] In his private letters, Gilson complained of the "anti-Thomists at the Council" and the new crop of "obnoxious seminarians" who made Aquinas "the symbol of everything that had to go."[47] In a similar fashion, Maritain's highly critical assessment of the postconciliar enthusiasm, articulated in his controversial book, *The Peasant of the Garonne* (1968), gave eloquent testimony to this sense of spiritual loss and alienation.[48]

Such criticisms laid the groundwork for oppositional movements of Catholic traditionalism and activist conservatism in the later decades of the twentieth century. They became the bases for what some would describe as movements of fundamentalism and right-wing schism in the Catholic Church.[49] Conservatives blamed radical activists for exaggerating the importance of the Council. Disenchanted liberals, who had fought to liberate Catholicism from American mediocrity, scored reformers for catering to the vulgarity of theological fashions. Converts, once attracted by the universality of the classical creeds and the Latin rite, charged Catholic pluralists with turning the church into a global confederacy of tribal churches. In its most extreme expression, anticonciliar dissent accused the Vatican Council of formal, if unintentional, heresy. It maintained that Pope John XXIII "spoke amiably about opening windows in his church while, actually and unwittingly, he was leveling the walls."[50]

In the immediate aftermath of the Second Vatican Council, what was left of the Catholic Revival movement suffered from identification with an outworn creed and an outdated mission. Heavily invested in what Franz Jozef van Beeck has called a "pistic" approach to faith—belief that seeks intellectual synthesis and authoritative definition—the Revival impulse appeared strange to progressive Catholics who were reinterpreting their tradition in terms of more charismatic and mystical models of faith experience.[51] In the categories of theologian George Lindbeck, the cognitive-propositional and cultural-linguistic varieties of faith characteristic of the Revival survived only as minority conceptions in a new atmosphere stressing the experiential and expressive dimensions of Christian life.[52] Privileging traditional formulations in continuity with the historic community's classical "rule of faith," the Revival spirituality found few adherents in a community newly engaged in the discovery of theological pluralism, ecumenical dialogue, and individual faith development.

Two consequences of the conciliar period had special significance for the demise of the Catholic Revival. The first was a disconcerting reversal in the church's commitment to the ideal of the lay intellectual. Despite its passage of a decree on the lay apostolate and its high praise for the laity in the dogmatic constitution on ecclesiology, *Lumen Gentium* (1964), the Council failed to advance the Revival's vision of lay intellectual life. While the Council raised the level of discussion regarding the laity to an unprecedented stage of development, it also represented a new level of clerical control over the course of that discussion, for only consecrated bishops possessed decision-making power at the Council. As priests and bishops became the official judges of the emerging theology of the laity, they muscled lay intellectuals out of the limelight. At the moment when official rhetoric regarding the expanded role of the laity was at its height, developments set in motion by the Council initiated what amounted to an ironic reclericalization of Catholic thought. Aside from work behind the scenes, loyal lay Catholics participated in the Council's official proceedings only as auditors. Lay women were not even allowed to join the delegation until 1964, during the third session. More importantly, the priest-theologians gaining international acclaim in the postconciliar era overshadowed the accomplishments of the great lay writers of the first half of the century. To a significant degree, Vatican II signaled the reappearance of the world-class priest-theologian for the first time since the death of Newman. The philosophical work of the controversial Jesuit scientist Pierre Teilhard de Chardin and the publications of the Council's expert theologians rendered earlier lay achievements obsolete. Conciliar consultants such as Hans Küng, Yves Congar, Jean Daniélou, Joseph Ratzinger, John Courtney Murray, and Karl Rahner dominated the intellectual scene once shared with eminent lay writers. Catapulted by the Council and the international press into unprecedented celebrity status, these "warrior-priests," according to historian H. Stuart Hughes, were perceived as members of a heroic "intellectual vanguard," giants on the world theological landscape dwarfing all previous inhabitants.[53] Meanwhile, Catholic Revival literature drifted out of print. For this reason, the staunchest opposition to the conciliar reforms often came from elite lay men and women who had received recognition in the lean years of Catholic intellectual activity when few professional theologians could have dreamed of reaching the fame of a Chesterton or a Belloc.[54]

As James Fisher has noted, for pioneers already engaged in the work of the lay apostolate, "the Council signaled an end more than a beginning."[55] According to Debra Campbell, the age of *aggiornamento* brought the lay renaissance of Catholic Action to a formal conclusion.[56] What Russell Jacoby has said about the vanishing public intellectual in American culture also applies to the lay writer and religious critic in post-Vatican II Catholicism.[57] As lay people made it into fields previously dominated by ordained priests—professional ministry and the specialized academic disciplines of philosophy, theology, and religious studies—little room was left for the lay public intellectual writing about issues of Catholic culture for the general educated audience. Furthermore, the violent turn of popular opinion against the intellectual vocation itself made the notion of an "intellectual apostolate" a liability in a democratizing Catholic community self-conscious about its new progressive image.[58] James Bacik's remark about the "virtual silence" currently surrounding the achievement of Maritain speaks to this shift in sensibility.[59] It was what left a demoralized Frank Sheed asking, "Why did the bright promise of the twenties, thirties and even forties, fade away into the sadness of the seventies?"[60]

A second trend of the postconciliar period presented a direct challenge to the Catholic Revival's distinctive *raison d'être*. As it gained momentum after the Council, the new Catholic spirituality showed little sympathy for the Revival's sense of memory and nostalgia. In fact, critics of the Revival singled out its cultivated sense of fondness for previous centuries in the church's experience, drawing close attention to the more atrocious qualities of medieval Christianity unworthy of modern emulation. In addition, the very notion of Christendom came under fire from theologians critical of the church's Constantinian legacy of entanglement with Western politics and its history of comfortable relations with culture.

Paradoxically, just as the international Catholic community claimed to be adopting an impressive hermeneutic of historical consciousness, the spiritual energies unleashed by enthusiasm over the Council seemed to engender a strange loss of historical perspective.[61] Some critics even argued that the church had too hastily exchanged its time-worn classicism for a blind loyalty to what Maritain called "chronolatry"—an uncritical captivity to contemporary standards.[62] For many conservative Catholics, the Council came to symbolize a plenary judgment on the immediate past, a ritual forgetting of the intellectual and cultural achievements that, arguably, had laid the foundation for the Council itself. Those with more Freudian tendencies detected in the postconciliar excitement the maniacal glee usually accompanying a "slaying of the fathers."[63]

Though certainly no father of the church, Tate shared Maritain's misgivings regarding the apparent trajectory of postconciliar Catholicism. The "neo-modernist" theological fads of the age concerned him and confirmed his suspicions of an emerging Catholic gnosticism. Especially irritated by the cult of popularity surrounding Teilhard (described by an exasperated Gilson as "the most Christian of the gnostics"), Tate once blasted a lay enthusiast of the Jesuit mystic, telling him in no uncertain terms to "shut up about Chardin."[64] At the same time, he chafed under the liturgical experimentation of the period and worried about the destructive effect of ecumenical ferment on Catholic devotion. As one who "got into the Church only through the Virgin," he was distressed by the tendency of the Vatican Council to "play down" Marian devotion in obvious overtures of friendship toward separated Protestant brethren. "If the Ecumenical movement is merely a levelling process towards 20th century rationalism," he prophesied during the second session of the Council, "it will fail."[65]

Attempting to describe the anxieties of that age of Catholic transition, James Fisher has recently produced a provocative portrait of convert Dorothy Day making her way into the old-fashioned Catholic subculture of personal piety and sacrificial obedience, precisely at the moment when her birthright Catholic followers, seeking to rid themselves of alien citizenship, were fleeing from the immigrant ghetto into the pluralism of America's secular city.[66] In a sense, Allen Tate was engaged in a similarly ill-timed pilgrimage. Walker Percy, fellow apologist for the forlorn values of the Catholic Revival, saw the plight of the modern Catholic writer as that of "a man who has found a treasure hidden in the attic of an old house, but [who] is writing for people who have moved out to the suburbs and who are bloody sick of the old house and everything in it."[67] To his dismay, Tate discovered the attic's treasure just as the house was going on the market. In his career, he witnessed not only the disappearance of the South's regional tradition in the wake of America's unrestrained march toward standardization but also the dissolution of what he perceived to be the best of Catholic tradition as well. To borrow a phrase from historian Mark Noll, Tate—as southerner and Catholic—joined the ranks of the twentieth century's "alienated losers twice over."[68]

Ora Pro Nobis

After his 1966 marriage to Helen Heinz, a trained nurse and former Catholic religious sister, Tate was eventually successful in regularizing his relationship to the Catholic Church.[69] For a brief season prior to his death, the wayward convert was reconciled to the sacramental life of his church. Though he never ceased to view himself as a believing Catholic, rarely did he ever speak again with the confidence of the committed convert. An evaporating cultural milieu coupled with his own internal moral struggles militated against faithful observance of his chosen religion. His, though, was not the familiar story of the ordinary lapsed believer, bothered by intellectual doubts or offended by ecclesiastical institutions. As *Renascence* editor Joseph Schwartz has observed, Tate was "a rotten Catholic, to use Hemingway's phrase, but a Catholic who never argued with the dogma or the authority of the Church. He just had a hard time leading a formal Catholic life."[70]

During a long tenure on the English faculty of the University of Minnesota and a decade of retirement in Tennessee, Tate continued to address religious issues in his critical work, as he persisted, with some uneasiness, in his search for the cultural incarnation of the West's classical religious humanism. In university lectures, he continued to identify the medieval vision of the liberal arts as the best model for Western higher education and to reject any humanist philosophy not ultimately grounded in theism.[71] His public discourse, however, lacked the authority once associated with dogmatic Catholic pronouncements on religion and culture. His 1969 lecture at Peabody College for Teachers in Nashville, for example, revealed the unsettled spirituality that marked his final years. On the perennial topic of faith and literature, *Mere Literature and the Lost Traveller* addressed the discomfiting fact of religion's "obscure" relation to art. Borrowing a conceit from William Blake, Tate compared himself to a traveller lost in a forest, who thinks he will get out by walking a straight line to the perimeter, but being right-handed always bears a little to the right, and after hours of fatigue returns to the place where he was first aware that he was lost.[72]

Ten years later, months of debilitating illness caught up with the listing wayfarer. After funeral rites at St. Henry's Catholic Church on the outskirts of Nashville, Tate was buried a hundred miles away in the family plot at Sewanee, Tennessee, home of the University of the South. The simple, obscure grave, surrounded by a low stone wall, contrasts sharply with Tate's stormy public career and the relentless labor of his religious quest. A witness to his stubborn creed, the tombstone's epitaph repeats the church's traditional Marian prayer: "*SANCTA MARIA ORA PRO NOBIS.*"

"Our Modern Unbelieving Belief"

Nearly all of the Revival's literary converts found their Catholic experience mixed with gain and loss. To their surprise, Catholic existence in what Karl Adam called the diaspora of Western culture still retained the shape of the "long wanderings and difficult inward crises of the western soul."[73] Chesterton and the Maritains, perhaps the most successful of them all, left their mark on a generation of Catholics but met their share of disappointment in the life of the church. For a variety of reasons, the "lost-generation" converts never fared very well either. Dorothy Day found the loneliness of the modern city a familiar reality inside the community of the church, and Thomas Merton discovered the chaos of the modern heart even in the silence of the monastic cloister. In her own words, Katherine Anne Porter, who thought her fellow literary converts "such a crashing bore," ended up calling herself a "mere backslider."[74] Her contemporary, Graham Greene, described himself as a "Catholic agnostic."[75] After a spurt of devotion in the late 1920s, Hemingway remained Catholic in name only. For his part, Tate placed his experience in what he called "our modern unbelieving belief."[76]

Literary historians have often wondered whether Allen Tate's "late acceptance of Catholicism came as an authentic conversion or as only the next step in his intellectual response" to the modern world's disturbing loss of tradition[77]—whether, that is, it was the sure decision of a veteran traveler or the panicky reflex of a restless fugitive. Some critics have suggested that Tate's self-confessed problems as a Catholic writer stemmed from awkward attempts to compensate for his failed experiment in Agrarianism or from his lifelong engagement with aesthetic modernism. Others have blamed the character of his Catholic experience on his chronic addiction to lost causes. One thing is certain: the question cannot be addressed adequately without an examination of the Catholic Revival's influence in Tate's work as a religious critic. The history of American Catholic intellectual life must come to terms with Tate's troubled Catholic quest in the context of an unraveling tradition of Catholic myth and meaning—an experience of Catholicism made not for all time but for an age.

Just prior to his baptism, Tate confessed:

> As I look back upon my own verse, written over more than twenty-five years, I see plainly that its main theme is man suffering from unbelief; and I cannot for a moment suppose that this man is some other than myself.[78]

Careful examination of his critical prose and his private writings reveals that one factor instrumental in Tate's retreat from that state of unbelief was his acquaintance with the literature, spirituality, and leadership of the Catholic Revival. Throughout the first phase of his career, over the course of a quarter century, as he looked for an enduring tradition to counter the negative effects of modernity and to sustain the internal requisites of his art, the intellectual ferment of the Catholic Literary Revival shaped Tate's personal understanding of Christianity as it molded his sympathies toward the church. Unlike other traditions, including his proud regional heritage, it seemed the only trustworthy alternative to the decadence of modernity.

A cunning convergence of personal and historical factors, however, rendered attraction to the Catholic Revival problematic for an intellectual convert like Tate. His conversion brought with it the ironic experience of spiritual displacement, for Tate entered a church engaged in a dramatic phase of reorientation and found himself lacking the spiritual constitution to weather the change wisely or well. His peculiar fate of living when a world was about to fall imperiled any possibility of easy belief or spiritual resolution. Lost in the dark wood of the twentieth century, his conversion marked Tate as a tireless pilgrim turning toward the fading light of a singular tradition of Catholic imagination, unable to discern whether the twilight promised dusk or dawn.

Notes

Introduction

1. Martin Heidegger, *Poetry, Language, Thought*, trans. Albert Hofstadter (New York: Harper and Row, 1971) 94.

2. Lem Coley, "Memories and Opinions of Allen Tate," *Southern Review* 28 (Autumn 1992): 963.

3. C. S. Lewis, *Surprised by Joy* (New York: Harcourt, Brace and World, 1955) 207.

④ Cf. Clarence Walhout and Leland Ryken, eds., *Contemporary* ✓ *Literary Theory: A Christian Appraisal* (Grand Rapids, MI: Eerdmans, 1991).

5. S. L. Weingart, "Cold Revery: Remembering Allen Tate," *Sewanee Review* 103 (Spring 1995): 281.

6. William Dean, *The Religious Critic in American Culture* (Albany: State University of New York Press, 1994).

7. John Tracy Ellis, "American Catholics and the Intellectual Life," *Thought* 30 (1955): 358, 381-382.

8. Jacques Maritain, letter to Mgr. R. Fontenelle, 24 August 1952, *Exiles and Fugitives: The Letters of Jacques and Raissa Maritain, Allen Tate, and Caroline Gordon*, ed. John M. Dunaway (Baton Rouge: Louisiana State University Press, 1992) 104.

9. Caroline Gordon, letter to Jacques Maritain, 18 October 1956, *Exiles and Fugitives* 62. William Lynch, letter to Allen Tate, 3 February 1953. Published with permission of the Manuscripts Division, Department of Rare Books and Special Collections, Princeton University Libraries. Hereafter cited as Princeton University Libraries.

10. Walter J. Ong, letter to Wilfred M. Mallon, 9 May 1953.

11. Marshall McLuhan, letter to Allen Tate, 2 October 1951. Princeton University Libraries.

12. Newman quoted in Brian Martin, *John Henry Newman: His Life and Work* (New York: Oxford University Press, 1982) 156.

13. Radcliffe Squires, letter to Allen Tate, 2 August 1967. Radcliffe Squires Papers, Washington University Libraries, St. Louis.

14. Walter Sullivan, *Allen Tate: A Recollection* (Baton Rouge: Louisiana State University Press, 1988) 110.

15. Allen Tate, letter to Robert Fitzgerald, 1 March 1952, *Exiles and Fugitives* 101.

16. John D. Barbour, *Versions of Deconversion: Autobiography and the Loss of Faith* (Charlottesville: University Press of Virginia, 1994).

17. Gary Wills, *Bare Ruined Choirs: Doubt, Prophecy, and Radical Religion* (Garden City, NY: Doubleday, 1972) 2.

18. Martin Heidegger, *Poetry, Language, Thought* 94.

19. Walter Allen, *Tradition and Dream: The English and American Novel from the Twenties to Our Time* (London: Readers Union, 1965) 124.

20. R. K. Meiners, *The Last Alternatives: A Study of the Works of Allen Tate* (Denver: Alan Swallow, 1963) 29.

21. Harold Bloom, *The American Religion: The Emergence of the Post-Christian Nation* (New York: Simon and Schuster, 1992) 21.

22. Hans Urs von Balthasar, *The Glory of the Lord: A Theological Aesthetics*, vol. 3, trans. Andrew Louth, John Saward, Martin Simon, and Rowan Williams (San Francisco: Ignatius Press, 1986).

23. C. Vann Woodward, *The Burden of Southern History* (New York: Vintage Books, 1961) 190.

24. Gene Burns, *The Frontiers of Catholicism: The Politics of Ideology in a Liberal World* (Berkeley: University of California Press, 1992) 17.

25. Cf. T. J. Jackson Lears, *No Place of Grace: Antimodernism and the Transformation of American Culture 1880–1920* (New York: Pantheon, 1981).

1. A World About to Fall

1. William James, *The Varieties of Religious Experience* (New York: Penguin, 1986) 328.

2. Allen Tate, *Essays of Four Decades* (Chicago: Swallow Press, 1968) 291-292, 288, 294.

3. Charles Reagan Wilson, *Baptized in Blood: The Religion of the Lost Cause, 1865–1920* (Athens: University of Georgia Press, 1980).

4. Eugene D. Genovese, *The Southern Tradition: The Achievement and Limitations of an American Conservatism* (Cambridge, MA: Harvard University Press, 1994).

5. Daniel Joseph Singal, *The War Within: From Victorian to Modernist Thought in the South, 1919–1945* (Chapel Hill: University of North Carolina Press, 1982) 254.

6. Allen Tate, letter to Donald Davidson, 18 February 1929, *The Literary Correspondence of Donald Davidson and Allen Tate*, ed. John Tyree

Fain and Thomas Daniel Young (Athens: University of Georgia Press, 1974) 223.

7. Allen Tate, *Memoirs and Opinions 1926–1974* (Chicago: Swallow Press, 1975) 190.

8. Jay P. Dolan, *The American Catholic Experience: A History from Colonial Times to the Present* (Garden City, NY: Image Books, 1985) 221-240.

9. Cf. Ann Taves, *The Household of Faith: Roman Catholic Devotions in Mid-Nineteenth Century America* (Notre Dame, IN: University of Notre Dame Press, 1986).

10. Roger Finke and Rodney Stark, *The Churching of America 1776–1990: Winners and Losers in Our Religious Economy* (New Brunswick, NJ: Rutgers University Press, 1992) 143, 115.

11. David O'Brien, *Public Catholicism* (New York: Macmillan, 1989) 124-194.

12. Cf. Arnold Sparr, "Chesterton and Catholic Moments: Some Reflections on Catholic Revivals, Past and Present," *Records of the American Catholic Historical Society of Philadelphia* 103 (Fall 1992): 11-22.

13. Dolores Elsie Brien, "The Catholic Revival Revisited," *Commonweal* 106 (21 December 1979): 714.

14. "The Catholic Revival," *Commonweal* 13 (4 March 1931): 478.

15. Cf. Wilfrid Ward, *William George Ward and the Catholic Revival* (1893; New York: Longmans, Green, 1912).

16. Hilaire Belloc, *Europe and the Faith* (London: Burns and Oates, 1962) 2.

17. Quentin Lauer, *G. K. Chesterton: Philosopher Without Porfolio* (New York: Fordham University Press, 1991).

18. Adrian Hastings, *A History of English Christianity 1920–1990* (London: SCM Press, 1991) 279-280.

19. James Hitchcock, "Postmortem on a Rebirth: The Catholic Intellectual Renaissance," *American Scholar* 49 (1980): 212.

20. Hilaire Belloc, *The Great Heresies* (Rockford, IL: TAN Books, 1991) 160.

21. Garry Wills, *Bare Ruined Choirs* 253.

22. Ronald Knox, *The Belief of Catholics* (Garden City, NY: Image Books, 1958) 29-30.

23. G. K. Chesterton, *The Innocence of Father Brown* (New York: Penguin, 1987) 52.

24. G. K. Chesterton, *The Man Who Was Thursday* (New York: Sheed and Ward, 1975) 17.

25. Calvert Alexander, *The Catholic Literary Revival* (Milwaukee: Bruce, 1935) 7, 10.

26. Cf. Jenny Franchot, *Roads to Rome: The Antebellum Protestant Encounter with Catholicism* (Berkeley: University of California, 1994).

27. John Tracy Ellis, "American Catholics and the Intellectual Life" 358.

28. Michael Williams, *Catholicism and the Modern Mind* (New York: Dial Press, 1928) 51.

29. "Catholic Converts," *Commonweal* 14 (6 May 1931): 5. The article reports 39,528 converts entering the Catholic Church in the United States during 1930.

30. Calvert Alexander, *The Catholic Literary Revival* 308.

31. Richard Gilman, *Faith, Sex, Mystery: A Memoir* (New York: Penguin, 1986) 168.

32. Raymond Nelson, *Van Wyck Brooks: A Writer's Life* (New York: E. P. Dutton, n.d.) 177. In *Intellectual Life In America: A History* (New York: Franklin Watts, 1984), Lewis Perry states that Lippmann considered conversion to Catholicism, "convinced that 'the acids of modernity' and the 'secular image of man' had dissolved social restraints and prepared the way for fascism and communism" (386).

33. George Santayana, *Winds of Doctrine and Platonism and the Spiritual Life* (New York: Harper Torchbooks, 1957) 49.

34. Thomas Merton, *The Seven Storey Mountain* (New York: Harcourt Brace Jovanovich, 1976) 175.

35. John Henry Newman, *Apologia Pro Vita Sua*, ed. David J. DeLaura (New York: W. W. Norton, 1968) 39.

36. Harold Bloom, introduction, *Modern Critical Views: Ernest Hemingway*, ed. Harold Bloom (New York: Chelsea House, 1985) 3.

37. William James, *The Varieties of Religious Experience* 460-461.

38. Anne Roche Muggeridge, *The Desolate City: Revolution in the Catholic Church*, rev. ed. (San Francisco: Harper, 1990) 7.

39. Thomas Merton, *New Seeds of Contemplation* (New York: New Directions, 1972) 84.

40. Thomas Merton, *The Seven Storey Mountain* 171ff.

41. Quoted in James Hennesey, *American Catholics: A History of the Roman Catholic Community in the United States* (Oxford: Oxford University Press, 1981) 255.

42. Leslie Woodcock Tentler, "On the Margins: The State of American Catholic History," *American Quarterly* 45 (March 1993): 113.

43. George Weigel, *Freedom and Its Discontents: Catholicism Confronts Modernity* (Washington, DC: Ethics and Public Policy Center, 1991) 139-143.

44. Arnold Sparr, *To Promote, Defend, and Redeem: The Catholic*

Literary Revival and the Cultural Transformation of American Catholicism, 1920–1960 (Westport, CT: Greenwood Press, 1990) xi-xii.

45. Arnold Sparr, *To Promote, Defend, and Redeem* 17-18.

46. George Shuster, *The Catholic Spirit in America* (New York: Dial Press, 1927). Michael Williams, *Catholicism and the Modern Mind*. Cf. Martin J. Bredeck, *Imperfect Apostles: "The Commonweal" and the American Catholic Laity, 1924–1976* (New York: Garland, 1988). Thomas E. Blantz, *George N. Shuster: On the Side of Truth* (Notre Dame, IN: University of Notre Dame Press, 1993).

47. John Pick, "The Renascence in American Catholic Letters," *The Catholic Renascence in a Disintegrating World*, ed. Norman Weyand (Chicago: Loyola University Press, 1951) 159.

48. Garry Wills, *Bare Ruined Choirs* 38-60.

49. Patrick W. Carey, "Lay Catholic Leadership in the United States," *U.S. Catholic Historian* 9 (Summer 1990): 238. Cf. Debra Campbell, "The Struggle to Serve: From the Lay Apostolate to the Ministry Explosion," *Transforming Parish Ministry: The Changing Roles of Catholic Clergy, Laity, and Women Religious*, Jay P. Dolan, et al. (New York: Crossroad, 1989) 201-280.

50. Philip C. Hoelle, "The Legion of Mary," pamphlet (Stockbridge, MA: Marian Apostolate, 1961) n.p.

51. Leslie Woodcock Tentler, "On the Margins: The State of American Catholic History" 118.

52. Cf. James K. Kenneally, *The History of American Catholic Women* (New York: Crossroad, 1990) 161-175.

53. Arnold Sparr, *To Promote, Defend, and Redeem* 99-142. John W. Meaney, *O'Malley of Notre Dame* (Notre Dame, IN: University of Notre Dame Press, 1991) 117-141. Cf. David Kubal, *The Consoling Intelligence: Responses to Literary Modernism* (Baton Rouge: Louisiana State University Press, 1982) 181-196.

54. R. W. Franklin and Robert L. Spaeth, *Virgil Michel: American Catholic* (Collegeville, MN: Liturgical Press, 1988) 145.

55. Arnold Sparr, *To Promote, Defend, and Redeem* 163-170.

56. Paul R. Messbarger, "The Failed Promise of American Catholic Literature," *U.S. Catholic Historian* 4 (1985): 147.

57. Jay P. Dolan, *The American Catholic Experience* 419-454.

58. Timothy G. McCarthy, *The Catholic Tradition: Before and After Vatican II, 1878–1993* (Chicago: Loyola University Press, 1994) 81.

59. Avery Dulles, *The Craft of Theology: From Symbol to System* (New York: Crossroad, 1992) vii.

60. James Terence Fisher, *The Catholic Counterculture in America 1933–1962* (Chapel Hill: University of North Carolina Press, 1989) 202.

61. Karl Rahner, "A Courageous Worldwide Theology," in Richard P. McBrien, *Catholicism*, 2 vols. (Minneapolis: Winston Press, 1980) 2: Appendix, xix.

62. Timothy G. McCarthy, *The Catholic Tradition* 81.

2. The Oldest Fundamentalism in the World

1. John Crowe Ransom, letter to Allen Tate, 6 May 1924, *Selected Letters of John Crowe Ransom*, ed. Thomas Daniel Young and George Core (Baton Rouge: Louisiana State University Press, 1985) 134.

2. Oswald Spengler, *The Decline of the West*, trans. Charles Francis Atkinson, 2 vols. (New York: Alfred A. Knopf, 1989).

3. Cf. T. J. Jackson Lears, *No Place of Grace*. See also Marshall Berman, *All That Is Solid Melts Into Air: The Experience of Modernity* (New York: Penguin, 1988).

4. Bakewell Morrison, *Revelation and the Modern Mind* (New York: Bruce, 1936) 21.

5. G. K. Chesterton, *The Man Who Was Thursday* 46.

6. Bakewell Morrison, *The Catholic Church and the Modern Mind* (New York: Bruce, 1933) 134. Morrison, *Revelation and the Modern Mind* 11, 20.

7. Cf. Arnold Lunn, *The Revolt Against Reason* (New York: Sheed and Ward, 1951).

8. Pius X, *Pascendi dominici gregis, The Papal Encyclicals 1903–1939*, ed. Claudia Carlen (Raleigh, NC: McGrath, 1981) 89.

9. Quoted in Gabriel Daly, *Transcendence and Immanence: A Study in Catholic Modernism and Integralism* (Oxford: Clarendon Press, 1980) 236.

10. Pius XI, *Ubi arcano dei consilio, The Papal Encyclicals 1903–1939* 237.

11. Cf. Michael V. Gannon, "Before and After Modernism: The Intellectual Isolation of the American Priest," *The Catholic Priest in the United States: Historical Investigations*, ed. John Tracy Ellis (Collegeville, MN: Saint John's University Press, 1971) 293-383. See also Patrick W. Carey, "American Catholicism and the Enlightenment Ethos," *Knowledge and Belief in America: Enlightenment Traditions and Modern Religious Thought*, ed. William M. Shea and Peter A. Huff (Cambridge: Cambridge University Press, 1995) 125-164.

12. Cf. Margaret Mary Reher, *Catholic Intellectual Life in America: A Historical Study of Persons and Movements* (New York: Macmillan, 1989) 94. R. Scott Appleby, *"Church and Age Unite!" The Modernist Impulse in American Catholicism* (Notre Dame, IN: University of Notre Dame Press, 1992) 53.

13. Gerald P. Fogarty, *American Catholic Biblical Scholarship: A History*

from the Early Republic to Vatican II (San Francisco: Harper and Row, 1989) 191. Cf. Joseph M. White, *The Diocesan Seminary in the United States: A History from the 1780s to the Present* (Notre Dame, IN: University of Notre Dame Press, 1989).

14. John C. Dwyer, *Church History: Twenty Centuries of Catholic Christianity* (New York: Paulist Press, 1985) 364. Cf. Lester R. Kurtz, *The Politics of Heresy: The Modernist Crisis in Roman Catholicism* (Berkeley: University of California Press, 1986). David G. Schultenover, *A View from Rome* (Bronx, NY: Fordham University Press, 1993).

15. Cf. James Hitchcock, "Postmortem on a Rebirth" 211-225.

16. James Hitchcock, *What Is Secular Humanism?* (Ann Arbor: Servant Books, 1982) 115-138.

17. Ronald Knox, *The Belief of Catholics* 20.

18. G. K. Chesterton, *Orthodoxy* (New York: Image Books, 1990) 158.

19. Thomas Merton, *New Seeds of Contemplation* 147.

20. John Hellman, "The Humanism of Jacques Maritain," *Understanding Maritain: Philosopher and Friend*, ed. Deal W. Hudson and Matthew J. Mancini (Macon, GA: Mercer University Press, 1987) 120.

21. Jacques Maritain, *Antimoderne* (Paris: Editions de la Revue des jeunes, 1922); *Three Reformers* (New York: Charles Scribner's Sons, 1929); *The Twilight of Civilization* (London: Sheed and Ward, 1946).

22. Jacques Maritain, *True Humanism*, trans. M. R. Adamson, 4th ed. (London: Geoffrey Bles, 1946) 108, 131. Cf. Brooke Williams Smith, *Jacques Maritain: Antimodern or Ultramodern? An Historical Analysis of His Critics, His Thought, and His Life* (New York: Oxford University Press; Amsterdam: Elsevier, 1976).

23. Christopher Dawson, *The Judgment of the Nations* (New York: Sheed and Ward, 1942) 7.

24. Calvert Alexander, *The Catholic Literary Revival* 4, 12, 308.

25. Cf. William M. Halsey, *The Survival of American Innocence: Catholicism in an Era of Disillusionment 1920–1940* (Notre Dame, IN: University of Notre Dame Press, 1980) 61-83. Philip Gleason, "American Catholics and the Mythic Middle Ages," *Keeping the Faith: American Catholicism Past and Present* (Notre Dame, IN: University of Notre Dame Press, 1989) 11-34. See also T. J. Jackson Lears, *No Place of Grace* 142-181.

26. R. H. Super, ed., *The Complete Prose Works of Matthew Arnold*, vol. 10 (Ann Arbor: University of Michigan Press, 1961–77) 165-166.

27. Jacques Maritain, *True Humanism* 121, 126, 238, 250, 203.

28. Allen Tate, lecture, Assumption University, 1958. Princeton University Libraries.

29. Allen Tate, letter to Radcliffe Squires, 2 February 1969. Radcliffe Squires Papers, Washington University Libraries, St. Louis. Allen Tate,

Mere Literature and the Lost Traveller (Nashville: George Peabody College for Teachers, 1969) n.p. Cf. Radcliffe Squires, *Allen Tate: A Literary Biography* (New York: Pegasus, 1971) 15.

30. Allen Tate, *Memoirs and Opinions* 6.

31. Ann Thompson and Eve Zibart, "The Poet's Poet: Reflections on Allen Tate," *Alumnews* (Summer 1992): 12.

32. John M. Bradbury, *The Fugitives: A Critical Account* (Chapel Hill: University of North Carolina Press, 1958) 10.

33. Cf. Paul K. Conkin, *Gone With the Ivy: A Biography of Vanderbilt University* (Knoxville: University of Tennessee Press, 1985).

34. Allen Tate, letter to John Gould Fletcher. Quoted in Daniel Joseph Singal, *The War Within* 403n.

35. John Crowe Ransom, letter to Allen Tate [Spring 1927], *Selected Letters of John Crowe Ransom* 168.

36. Allen Tate, *Mere Literature and the Lost Traveller* n.p.

37. Allen Tate, letter to Donald Davidson, 21 July 1922, *The Literary Correspondence of Donald Davidson and Allen Tate* 20.

38. Cf. Louise Cowan, *The Fugitive Group: A Literary History* (Baton Rouge: Louisiana State University Press, 1959). Louis D. Rubin, Jr., *The Wary Fugitives: Four Poets and the South* (Baton Rouge: Louisiana State University Press, 1978).

39. Allen Tate, *Memoirs and Opinions* 24-34.

40. After the *Fugitive* began publication, women writers, such as Laura Riding Gottschalk, Ellen Grimes, and Katherine Estes Rice, contributed to the magazine, but were never considered members of the inner circle of the group.

41. A. N. Wilson, *C. S. Lewis: A Biography* (New York: W. W. Norton, 1990) xii.

42. See the Foreword to the first issue of the *Fugitive* (April 1922) in *The Fugitive* (Gloucester, MA: Peter Smith, 1967).

43. Langdon Hammer, *Hart Crane and Allen Tate: Janus-Faced Modernism* (Princeton: Princeton University Press, 1993) xi.

44. John Crowe Ransom, "In Amicitia," *Sewanee Review* 67 (October-December 1959): 531.

45. Donald Davidson, letter to Allen Tate, 23 August 1922, *The Literary Correspondence of Donald Davidson and Allen Tate* 38.

46. Donald Davidson, letter to Allen Tate, 29 August 1922, *The Literary Correspondence of Donald Davidson and Allen Tate* 43. Cf. John Crowe Ransom, letter to Allen Tate, 17 December 1922, *Selected Letters of John Crowe Ransom* 114-116.

47. T. S. Eliot, *Selected Prose of T. S. Eliot*, ed. Frank Kermode (New York: Harcourt Brace Jovanovich, Farrar, Straus and Giroux, 1975) 43, 40, 38.

48. Quoted in Angus Calder, *T. S. Eliot* (Atlantic Highlands, NJ: Humanities Press International, 1987) 161.

49. Wyndham Lewis, *Hitler* (London: Chatto and Windus, 1931). Ezra Pound *Jefferson and/or Mussolini* (New York: Liveright, 1970).

50. Cf. Gene Edward Veith, Jr., *Modern Fascism: Liquidating the Judeo-Christian Worldview* (St. Louis: Concordia, 1993) 115-118. See also Cairns Craig, *Yeats, Eliot, Pound, and the Politics of Poetry* (Pittsburgh: University of Pittsburgh Press, 1982).

51. T. S. Eliot, *For Lancelot Andrewes: Essays on Style and Order* (London: Faber and Faber, 1970) 7.

52. T. S. Eliot, *After Strange Gods: A Primer of Modern Heresy* (New York: Harcourt, Brace and Company, 1934) 20, 12.

53. Quoted in Alfred Kazin, *On Native Grounds* (San Diego: Harcourt Brace Jovanovich, 1982) 402.

54. Langdon Hammer, *Hart Crane and Allen Tate* 3-30.

55. Quoted in George H. Nash, *The Conservative Intellectual Movement in America Since 1945* (New York: Basic Books, 1976) 57.

56. Allen Tate, letter to Donald Davidson, 5 February 1933. Quoted in Daniel Joseph Singal, *The War Within* 252.

57. Albert J. Montesi, *The Creation of a Period Style: Modern Poetry 1900–1950*, unpublished manuscript, 84.

58. Allen Tate, letter to Donald Davidson, 8 July 1925, *The Literary Correspondence of Donald Davidson and Allen Tate* 141.

59. T. S. Eliot, "Religion and Literature," *Selected Prose of T. S. Eliot* 97.

60. Donald Davidson, letter to Allen Tate, 29 July 1929, *The Literary Correspondence of Donald Davidson and Allen Tate* 227.

61. Paul K. Conkin, *The Southern Agrarians* (Knoxville: University of Tennessee Press, 1988).

62. Cf. Morton and Lucia White, *The Intellectual Versus the City: From Thomas Jefferson to Frank Lloyd Wright* (Oxford: Oxford University Press, 1977). Robert L. Dorman, *Revolt of the Provinces: The Regionalist Movement in America, 1920–1945* (Chapel Hill: University of North Carolina Press, 1993). David E. Shi, *The Simple Life: Plain Living and High Thinking in American Culture* (New York: Oxford University Press, 1985).

63. Twelve Southerners, *I'll Take My Stand: The South and the Agrarian Tradition* (Baton Rouge: Louisiana State University Press, 1977). Herbert Agar and Allen Tate, eds., *Who Owns America? A New Declaration of Independence* (Boston: Houghton Mifflin, 1936).

64. Quoted from the first version of the Agrarian "Statement of Principles" in Virginia J. Rock, "The Making and Meaning of *I'll Take My Stand*: A Study in Utopian Conservatism, 1925–1939," diss., University of Minnesota, 1961, 465.

65. Virginia Rock, "The Making and Meaning of *I'll Take My Stand*" 421-422.

66. Allen Tate, "Remarks on the Southern Religion," *I'll Take My Stand* 168. John Crowe Ransom, *God Without Thunder: An Unorthodox Defense of Orthodoxy* (Hamden, CT: Archon Books, 1965) 116.

67. Cf. Thomas Daniel Young, "From Fugitives to Agrarians," *Mississippi Quarterly* 33 (Fall 1980): 420-424.

68. Cf. Daniel Joseph Singal, *The War Within* 200-201, 398n. See also Paul K. Conkin, *The Southern Agrarians* 24ff.

69. Rob Roy Purdy, ed., *Fugitives' Reunion: Conversations at Vanderbilt, May 3–5, 1956* (Nashville: Vanderbilt University Press, 1959) 199. See also Andrew Lytle, "They Took Their Stand: The Agrarian View After Fifty Years," *Modern Age* 24 (Spring 1980): 116.

70. Donald Davidson, *Southern Writers in the Modern World* (Athens: University of Georgia Press, 1958) 30, 40.

71. Henry F. May, *The End of American Innocence* (Chicago: Quadrangle Books, 1964) 129n. Cf. William R. Hutchison, *The Modernist Impulse in American Protestantism* (Durham: Duke University Press, 1992) 257-287.

72. H. Richard Niebuhr, *The Social Sources of Denominationalism* (Cleveland: Meridian Books, 1968) 184-186.

73. Cf. George M. Marsden, *Fundamentalism and American Culture: The Shaping of Twentieth-Century Evangelicalism 1870–1925* (Oxford: Oxford University Press, 1980) 179, 188, 202.

74. George M. Marsden, *Understanding Fundamentalism and Evangelicalism* (Grand Rapids, MI: Eerdmans, 1991) 200. R. Laurence Moore, *Religious Outsiders and the Making of Americans* (New York: Oxford University Press, 1986) 163.

75. Donald Davidson, *Southern Writers in the Modern World* 34.

76. Donald Davidson, "The Artist as Southerner," *Saturday Review of Literature* (May 15, 1926): 782-783.

77. J. Gresham Machen, *Christianity and Liberalism* (Grand Rapids, MI: Eerdmans, 1946) 15.

78. Cf. Peter Huff, "Donald Davidson and 'America's Other Lost Generation,'" *Modern Age* 37 (Spring 1995): 226-232.

79. Stark Young, "Not in Memoriam, But in Defence," *I'll Take My Stand* 341.

80. Andrew Lytle, "The Hind Tit," *I'll Take My Stand* 244-245.

81. Rob Roy Purdy, ed., *Fugitives' Reunion* 181.

82. Cf. Edwin Mims, *The Advancing South: Stories of Progress and Reaction* (Port Washington, NY: Kennikat, 1969) xi, 279ff. Chancellor James H. Kirkland quoted in Sarah Newman Shouse, *Hillbilly Realist: Herman Clarence Nixon of Possum Trot* (University: University of Alabama Press, 1986) 44.

83. Cf. Kieran Quinlan, *John Crowe Ransom's Secular Faith* (Baton Rouge: Louisiana State University Press, 1989).

84. George Santayana, *Interpretations of Poetry and Religion* (Gloucester, MA: Peter Smith, 1969) 98.

85. John Crowe Ransom, *God Without Thunder* 81, 215, 11.

86. William M. Shea, *The Naturalists and the Supernatural: Studies in Horizon and an American Philosophy of Religion* (Macon, GA: Mercer University Press, 1984) 93. Cf. Sigmund Freud, *The Future of an Illusion*, trans. James Strachey (New York: W. W. Norton, 1989) 41.

87. George Santayana, *Winds of Doctrine and Platonism and the Spiritual Life* 39.

88. John Crowe Ransom, *God Without Thunder* 95-99.

89. Malcolm Cowley, *Exile's Return: A Literary Odyssey of the 1920's* (New York: Viking Press, 1956).

90. Cf. Allen Tate, "Random Thoughts on the 1920's," *Minnesota Review* 1 (Fall 1960): 46-56 and *Memoirs and Opinions* 46-68.

91. Allen Tate, "Last Days of the Charming Lady," *Nation* 121 (28 October 1925): 485.

92. Quoted in Alex Karanikas, *Tillers of a Myth: Southern Agrarians as Social and Literary Critics* (Madison: University of Wisconsin Press, 1966) 19.

93. Irv Broughton, "An Interview with Allen Tate," *Western Humanities Review* 32 (1978): 329.

94. Andrew Lytle, "They Took Their Stand" 116.

95. Irv Broughton, "An Interview with Allen Tate" 329.

96. Allen Tate, *Essays of Four Decades* 545. Allen Tate, *Collected Poems 1919–1976* (Baton Rouge: Louisiana State University Press, 1989) 21. To Davidson, Tate wrote, "My attempt is to see the present from the past, yet remain immersed in the present and committed to it" (20 February 1927, *The Literary Correspondence of Donald Davidson and Allen Tate* 189).

97. Allen Tate, *The Poetry Reviews of Allen Tate, 1924–1944*, ed. Ashley Brown and Frances Neel Cheney (Baton Rouge: Louisiana State University Press, 1983) 88.

98. Allen Tate, "Whose Ox?" *Fugitive* 1 (December 1922): 99.

99. Allen Tate, "One Escape from the Dilemma," *Fugitive* 3 (April 1924): 35-36.

100. Allen Tate, letter to Donald Davidson, 14 May 1926, *The Literary Correspondence of Donald Davidson and Allen Tate* 166.

101. Allen Tate, "The Revolt Against Literature," *New Republic* 49 (9 February 1927): 330.

102. Marshall Berman, *All That Is Solid Melts Into Air* 28, 169.

103. Allen Tate, "The Same Fallacy of Humanism: A Reply to Mr. Robert Shafer," *Bookman* 71 (March 1930): 33.

104. Robert S. Dupree, *Allen Tate and the Augustinian Imagination: A Study of the Poetry* (Baton Rouge: Louisiana State University Press, 1983) 23-29.

105. Allen Tate, "Fundamentalism," *Nation* 122 (12 May 1926): 532-534.

106. Allen Tate, letter to Donald Davidson, 3 March 1926, *The Literary Correspondence of Donald Davidson and Allen Tate* 158.

107. Allen Tate, letter to Donald Davidson, 5 May 1927, *The Literary Correspondence of Donald Davidson and Allen Tate* 200.

108. Charles Reagan Wilson, "God's Project: The Southern Civil Religion, 1920–1980," *Religion and the Life of the Nation*, ed. Rowland A. Sherrill (Urbana: University of Illinois Press, 1990) 67-70.

109. Allen Tate, *Stonewall Jackson: The Good Soldier* (Nashville: J. S. Sanders, 1991) 11, 125.

110. Allen Tate, *Jefferson Davis: His Rise and Fall* (New York: Minton, Balch, 1929) 87.

111. Walter J. Ong, *Frontiers in American Catholicism* (New York: Macmillan, 1957) 35.

112. Allen Tate, *Jefferson Davis* 154-176.

113. Walter Lippmann, *A Preface to Morals* (New York: Time, 1964) 33.

114. Allen Tate, *Memoirs and Opinions* 50-52.

115. Christopher Hollis, *The American Heresy* (London: Sheed and Ward, 1927) 9. Tate called Hollis "the ablest defender the South has had since Dew, Harper, and Calhoun." See Allen Tate, letter to Donald Davidson, 12 April 1928, *The Literary Correspondence of Donald Davidson and Allen Tate* 212-213.

116. Allen Tate, letter to Andrew Lytle, 31 July 1929, *The Lytle-Tate Letters: The Correspondence of Andrew Lytle and Allen Tate*, ed. Thomas Daniel Young and Elizabeth Sarcone (Jackson: University Press of Mississippi, 1987) 34.

117. Allen Tate, *Stonewall Jackson* 45-46 and *Jefferson Davis* 59. Tate neglected to state that the young Jefferson Davis also briefly flirted

with the notion of converting to Catholicism. Cf. Varina Davis, *Jefferson Davis: A Memoir by his Wife*, 2 vols. (Baltimore: Nautical and Aviation Publishing Company, 1990) 1: 13-14.

118. Allen Tate, *Memoirs and Opinions* 190.

119. Irving Babbitt, *Democracy and Leadership* (Boston: Houghton Mifflin, 1925) 186.

120. Allen Tate, letter to Donald Davidson, 10 August 1929, *The Literary Correspondence of Donald Davidson and Allen Tate* 230. Cf. Allen Tate, letter to Andrew Lytle, 31 July 1929, *The Lytle-Tate Letters* 34.

121. Allen Tate, letter to Donald Davidson, 18 February 1929, *The Literary Correspondence of Donald Davidson and Allen Tate* 223-224.

122. Joseph Schopp, *Allen Tate: Tradition als Bauprinzip dualistischen Dichtens* (Bonn: Bouvier Verlag Herbert Grundmann, 1975) 68-91.

123. Allen Tate, *Memoirs and Opinions* 190-191.

124. Allen Tate, letter to Donald Davidson, undated. Quoted in Virginia Rock, "The Making and Meaning of *I'll Take My Stand*" 288. Tate's early prospectus for the essay stated, "In this essay Fundamentalism is defended and Dayton explained historically." Proposed Table of Contents for *I'll Take My Stand*. Donald Davidson Papers. Vanderbilt University Library.

125. Allen Tate, "Remarks on the Southern Religion," *I'll Take My Stand* 168, cf. 166, 173-174.

126. Quoted in C. B. Wilmer, "Mr. Allen Tate Wants to Know," *Atlanta Journal* (8 February 1931).

127. Allen Tate, "A View of the Whole South," *American Review* 2 (February 1934): 426.

128. Allen Tate, *Essays of Four Decades* 521.

3. The Cause of the Land

1. Quoted in John Tytell, *Ezra Pound: The Solitary Volcano* (New York: Anchor Press, 1987) 299.

2. G. K. Chesterton, *All Is Grist* (London: Methuen, 1931) 49, 53.

3. David J. O'Brien, *American Catholics and Social Reform: The New Deal Years* (New York: Oxford University Press, 1968) 102.

4. Pius XI called *Rerum novarum* "the *Magna Charta* upon which all Christian activity in the social field ought to be based." Pius XI, *Quadragesimo anno*, *The Papal Encyclicals 1903-1939* 421.

5. Leo XIII, *Rerum novarum*, *The Papal Encyclicals 1878–1903*, ed. Claudia Carlen (Raleigh, NC: McGrath, 1981) 243, 248.

6. Pius XI, *Quadragesimo anno*, *The Papal Encyclicals 1903–1939* 420, 422, 428.

7. Cf. Joseph C. Husslein, *The Christian Social Manifesto: An Interpretative Study of the Encyclicals "Rerum novarum" and "Quadragesimo anno" of Pope Leo XIII and Pope Pius XI*, rev. ed. (Milwaukee: Bruce, 1939).

8. Gene Burns, *The Frontiers of Catholicism: The Politics of Ideology in a Liberal World* 31, 37.

9. Cf. John P. McCarthy, *Hilaire Belloc: Edwardian Radical* (Indianapolis: Liberty Press, 1978). Margaret Canovan, *G. K. Chesterton: Radical Populist* (New York: Harcourt Brace Jovanovich, 1977).

10. Hilaire Belloc, *The Servile State* (New York: Henry Holt and Company, 1946) 51, 183. Cf. Belloc's article on "Land-Tenure in the Christian Era" in *The Catholic Encyclopedia*, 15 vols. (New York: Robert Appleton, 1907–1912) 8: 775-784. See also G. K. Chesterton, *A Short History of England* (London: Chatto and Windus, 1920).

11. Hilaire Belloc, *The Servile State* 57-77, 187-189 and *The Restoration of Property* (New York: Sheed and Ward, 1936) 41, 105, 62.

12. Quoted in Michael Finch, *G. K. Chesterton: A Biography* (San Francisco: Harper and Row, 1986) 276.

13. G. K. Chesterton, *The Outline of Sanity* (London: Methuen, 1926) 170, 228.

14. Cf. Quentin Lauer, *G. K. Chesterton: Philosopher Without Portfolio* 111-146.

15. Jay P. Corrin, *G. K. Chesterton and Hilaire Belloc: The Battle Against Modernity* (Athens: Ohio University Press, 1981) xiii.

16. *Flee to the Fields: The Faith and Works of the Catholic Land Movement* (London: Heath Cranton, 1934).

17. A. N. Wilson, *Hilaire Belloc: A Biography* (New York: Atheneum, 1984) 117.

18. Cf. Fiona MacCarthy, *Eric Gill* (New York: E. P. Dutton, 1989).

19. Maisie Ward, *Unfinished Business* (New York: Sheed and Ward, 1964) 145-152.

20. Cf. Ferdinand Valentine, *Father Vincent McNabb, O.P.* (London: Burns and Oates, 1955).

21. Quoted in Martin E. Schirber, "American Catholicism and Life on the Land," *Social Order* 12 (May 1962): 204.

22. Rosemary Haughton quoted in Timothy Michael Dolan, *"Some Seed Fell on Good Ground": The Life of Edwin V. O'Hara* (Washington, DC: Catholic University of America, 1992) 104.

23. Cf. M. Thomas Inge, ed., *Agrarianism in American Literature* (New York: Odyssey, 1969). James Montmarquet, *The Idea of Agrarianism: From Hunter Gatherer to Agrarian Radical in Western Culture* (Moscow:

University of Idaho Press, 1989). Arthur Ekirch, Jr., *Man and Nature in America* (New York: Columbia University Press, 1963).

24. Peter J. Schmitt, *Back to Nature: The Arcadian Myth in Urban America* (New York: Oxford University Press, 1969).

25. Edward S. Shapiro, "The Catholic Rural Life Movement and the New Deal Farm Program," *American Benedictine Review* 28 (September 1977): 310.

26. Jan Wojcik, "The American Wisdom Literature of Farming," *Agriculture and Human Values* 1 (Fall 1984): 26-37.

27. Cf. Robert C. McMath, Jr., *American Populism: A Social History 1877–1898* (New York: Hill and Wang, 1993).

28. Thomas J. Lyon, ed., *This Incomperable Lande: A Book of American Nature Writing* (New York: Penguin, 1989) 86-87.

29. William L. Bowers, *The Country Life Movement in America, 1900–1920* (Port Washington, NY: Kennikat Press, 1974).

30. David B. Danbom, "Romantic Agrarianism in Twentieth-Century America," *Agricultural History* 65 (Fall 1991): 7.

31. Ralph Borsodi, *This Ugly Civilization* (New York: Simon and Schuster, 1929) 459-462.

32. Cf. Liberty Hyde Bailey, *The Holy Earth* (New York: Christian Rural Fellowship, 1943).

33. Mark Rich, *The Rural Church Movement* (Columbia: University of Missouri, 1957). Merwin Swanson, "The 'Country Life Movement' and the American Churches," *Church History* 45 (September 1977): 358-373.

34. Lefferts A. Loetscher, *A Brief History of the Presbyterians*, 4th ed. (Philadelphia: Westminster Press, 1983) 134. Cf. *Report of the Commission on Country Life*, with an introduction by Theodore Roosevelt (New York: Sturgis and Walton, 1911).

35. Cf. Victor I. Masters, *Country Church in the South* (Atlanta: Home Mission Board, 1916) and *Making America Christian* (Atlanta: Home Mission Board, 1921).

36. Walter Rauschenbusch, *Christianity and the Social Crisis*, ed. Robert D. Cross (New York: Harper Torchbooks, 1964) 221.

37. Jenkin Lloyd Jones, *The Agricultural Social Gospel in America: The Gospel of the Farm*, ed. Thomas E. Graham (Lewiston, NY: Edwin Mellen Press, 1986).

38. Jay Dolan, *The Immigrant Church: New York's Irish and German Catholics, 1815–1865* (Notre Dame, IN: University of Notre Dame Press, 1983) 133-140.

39. Martin E. Schirber, "American Catholicism and Life on the Land" 193.

40. Christopher J. Kauffman, *Mission to Rural America: The Story of W.*

Howard Bishop, Founder of Glenmary (New York: Paulist Press, 1991) 59-74.

41. Timothy Michael Dolan, *"Some Seed Fell on Good Ground": The Life of Edwin V. O'Hara* 58-110, cf. 126-155.

42. National Catholic Rural Life Conference, *Manifesto on Rural Life* (Milwaukee: Bruce, 1939) v.

43. Cf. Edward S. Shapiro, "Catholic Agrarian Thought and the New Deal," *Modern American Catholicism, 1900–1965,* ed. Edward R. Kantowicz (New York: Garland, 1988) 583-599.

44. Cf. Christopher Kauffman, *Mission to Rural America* 105ff. Vincent A. Yzermans, *The People I Love: A Biography of Luigi G. Ligutti* (Collegeville, MN: Liturgical Press, 1976).

45. Raymond Philip Witte, *Twenty-Five Years of Crusading: A History of the National Catholic Rural Life Conference* (Des Moines: National Catholic Rural Life Conference, 1948) 212-215. Cf. Vincent A. Yzermans, "The National Catholic Rural Life Conference," *Catholics in America, 1776–1976,* ed. Robert Trisco (Washington, DC: National Council of Catholic Bishops, 1976).

46. Cf. *The Social Question: Essays on Capitalism and Christianity by Fr. Virgil Michel, O.S.B.,* ed. Robert L. Spaeth (Collegeville, MN: St. John's University, 1987).

47. Raymond P. Witte, *Twenty-Five Years of Crusading* 209. Cf. Gilbert J. Garraghan, *The Jesuits of the Middle United States,* 3 vols. (New York: America Press, 1938) 3: 448-450.

48. Peter McDonough, *Men Astutely Trained: A History of the Jesuits in the American Century* (New York: Free Press, 1992) 65-97.

49. Abigail McCarthy, *Private Faces/Public Places* (New York: Curtis Books, 1972) 109, 118, 123.

50. Cf. Wilfrid Sheed, *Frank and Maisie: A Memoir with Parents* (New York: Simon and Schuster, 1985) 209-211. See also Maisie Ward, ed., *Be Not Solicitous: Sidelights on the Providence of God and the Catholic Family* (New York: Sheed and Ward, 1954) 3-54, 208-254.

51. Cf. Mel Piehl, *Breaking Bread: The Catholic Worker and the Origin of Catholic Radicalism in America* (Philadelphia: Temple University Press, 1982).

52. Belden C. Lane, *Landscapes of the Sacred: Geography and Narrative in American Spirituality* (New York: Paulist Press, 1988) 174, 167.

53. Peter Maurin, *Easy Essays* (Chicago: Franciscan Herald Press, 1977) 129, cf. 171.

54. Dorothy Day, *Loaves and Fishes: The Story of the Catholic Worker Movement* (San Francisco: Harper and Row, 1983) 49.

55. Cf. Mary C. Segers, "Equality and Christian Anarchism: The Political and Social Ideas of the Catholic Worker Movement," *Modern American Catholicism, 1900–1965* 196-230. James Terence Fisher, *The Catholic Counterculture in America* 1-99.

56. Anthony Novitsky, "Peter Maurin's Green Revolution: The Radical Implications of Reactionary Social Catholicism," *Review of Politics* 37 (1975): 83-103.

57. Peter Maurin, *Easy Essays* 111.

58. Edward S. Shapiro, "The Catholic Rural Life Movement and the New Deal Farm Movement" 310. Cf. Edward S. Shapiro, "Decentralist Intellectuals and the New Deal," *Journal of American History* 58 (March 1972): 938-957.

59. Cf. Allen Tate, letter to Donald Davidson, 12 April 1928, *The Literary Correspondence of Donald Davidson and Allen Tate* 212. The disputed phrase "utopian conservatism" is from Virginia J. Rock, "The Making and Meaning of *I'll Take My Stand*: A Study in Utopian Conservatism, 1925-1939."

60. Allen Tate, "Remarks on the Southern Religion," *I'll Take My Stand* 166, 168.

61. Allen Tate, letter to Donald Davidson, 10 August 1929, *The Literary Correspondence of Donald Davidson and Allen Tate* 232.

62. Donald Davidson, letter to Allen Tate, 26 October 1929, *The Literary Correspondence of Donald Davidson and Allen Tate* 236.

63. Allen Tate, letter to Donald Davidson, 11 December 1929, *The Literary Correspondence of Donald Davidson and Allen Tate* 242, cf. 240. For biographical information on Dixon Wecter, see *The American Catholic Who's Who: 1938 and 1939* (Detroit: Walter Romig, 1939) 3: 443.

64. Cf. John L. Stewart, *The Burden of Time: The Fugitives and Agrarians* (Princeton: Princeton University Press, 1965) 133-135, 163, 167.

65. Allen Tate, letter to Contributors to the Southern Symposium, 24 July 1930, *The Literary Correspondence of Donald Davidson and Allen Tate* 406.

66. Allen Tate, "Remarks on the Southern Religion," *I'll Take My Stand* 155n.

67. Paul K. Conkin, *The Southern Agrarians* 71-72.

68. Allen Tate, "Remarks on the Southern Religion," *I'll Take My Stand* 175, 174.

69. Allen Tate, "Remarks on the Southern Religion," *I'll Take My Stand* 169.

70. Quoted in Thomas Daniel Young, *Gentleman in a Dustcoat: A Biography of John Crowe Ransom* (Baton Rouge: Louisiana State University Press, 1976) 244.

71. T. S. Eliot, *After Strange Gods* 53, 21n. Later, in the Prefaces to *The Idea of a Christian Society* (New York: Harcourt, Brace, and Company, 1940) and *Notes Toward the Definition of Culture* (New York: Harcourt, Brace, and Company, 1949), Eliot acknowledged his continuing dependence upon the thought of Christopher Dawson and others associated with the social thought of the Catholic Revival.

72. "Editorial Notes," *American Review* 1 (April 1933): 126. Cf. Albert E. Stone, "Seward Collins and the *American Review*: Experiment in Pro-Fascism, 1933–1937," *American Quarterly* 12 (Spring 1960): 3-19.

73. Samuel Eliot Morison, *The Oxford History of the American People* (New York: Oxford University Press, 1965) 970.

74. Allen Tate, "The Problem of the Unemployed," *American Review* 1 (May 1933): 129-149 and "What is a Traditional Society?" *American Review* 7 (September 1936): 376-387.

75. Cf. G. K. Chesterton, "The Day of the Lord," *American Review* 1 (April 1933): 76-79 and "The Masterless Man," *American Review* 3 (June 1934): 327-330. Hilaire Belloc, "The Restoration of Property," *American Review* 1 (April 1933): 1-16; 1 (May 1933): 204-219; 1 (June 1933): 344-357; 1 (September 1933): 468-482; 1 (October 1933): 600-609.

76. "Editorial Notes," *American Review* 2 (November 1933): 122.

77. Seward Collins, letter to Allen Tate, 18 April 1933. Princeton University Libraries.

78. Cf. Allen Tate, *Essays of Four Decades* 32, 200 and *Reason in Madness* (Salem, NH: Ayer, 1988) 205.

79. Allen Tate, letter to John Peale Bishop, 7 April 1933, *The Republic of Letters in America: The Correspondence of John Peale Bishop and Allen Tate*, ed. Thomas Daniel Young and John J. Hindle (Lexington: University Press of Kentucky, 1981) 77.

80. Christopher J. Kauffman, *Mission to Rural America* 98-99.

81. Allen Tate, letter to Herbert Agar, 9 September 1933. Princeton University Libraries.

82. Allen Tate, letter to Herbert Agar, 17 November 1933. Princeton University Libraries.

83. Allen Tate, letter to Eugene F. Saxton, 14 October 1933 (never sent). Princeton University Libraries.

84. Allen Tate, letter to Eugene F. Saxton, 17 November 1933, *The Literary Correspondence of Donald Davidson and Allen Tate* 409-411.

85. Herbert Agar, introduction, *Who Owns America?* ix.

86. Herbert Agar and Allen Tate, eds., *Who Owns America?* 194-214, 334-342, 36-51.

87. Herbert Agar, letter to Allen Tate, 1 April 1936. Princeton University Libraries.

88. Peter McDonough, *Men Astutely Trained* 95.

89. John C. Rawe, "Agrarianism: An Economic Foundation," *Modern Schoolman* 13 (November 1935): 15-20; "The Agrarian Concept of Property," *Modern Schoolman* 14 (November 1936): 4-6; "The Modern Homestead," *Modern Schoolman* 15 (January 1938): 33-36; "Biological Technology on the Land," *Catholic Rural Life Bulletin* 2 (20 August 1939): 1-3, 20-22. Luigi G. Ligutti and John C. Rawe, *Rural Roads to Security: America's Third Struggle for Freedom* (Milwaukee: Bruce, 1940).

90. Cf. R. A. McGowan, "Independence and Interdependence," *Commonweal* 24 (12 June 1936): 191-193.

91. Herbert Agar, letter to Allen Tate and Andrew Lytle, 22 December 1936. Princeton University Libraries.

92. Herbert Agar, letter to Allen Tate, 4 January 1936; letter to Chard Powers Smith, 13 April 1936. Princeton University Libraries. Cf. Cleanth Brooks, "The Christianity of Modernism," *American Review* 6 (February 1936): 435-446 and "A Plea to the Protestant Churches," *Who Owns America?* 323-333.

93. Minutes of the Convention of the Committee for the Alliance of Agrarian and Distributist Groups in Nashville, Tennessee, 4-5 June 1936. Andrew Nelson Lytle Papers, Vanderbilt University Library.

94. Cf. Peter McDonough, *Men Astutely Trained* 518n.

95. Paul Conkin, *The Southern Agrarians* 124-126.

96. Baker Brounell, letter to Allen Tate, 2 March 1937. Princeton University Libraries.

97. Allen Tate, letter to Donald Davidson, 23 February 1936, *The Literary Correspondence of Donald Davidson and Allen Tate* 296-297.

98. Allen Tate, letter to Herbert Agar, 9 December 1936. Princeton University Libraries.

99. Allen Tate, letter to Donald Davidson, 28 September 1935, *The Literary Correspondence of Donald Davidson and Allen Tate*, 294.

100. Paul Conkin, *The Southern Agrarians* 126.

101. Allen Tate, "A Personal Statement on Fascism." Princeton University Libraries.

102. Cf. Robert Shafer, "Humanism and Impudence," *Bookman* 70 (January 1930): 491; Allen Tate, "The Same Fallacy of Humanism," *Bookman* 71 (March 1930): 31. See also Allen Tate, "A Traditionalist Looks at Liberalism," *Southern Review* 1 (Spring 1936): 731-744;

reprinted as "Liberalism and Traditionalism" in *Reason in Madness* 196-216.

103. Christopher Dawson, letters to Alan Tait (sic), 26 April 1940, 27 August 1940. Princeton University Libraries.

104. Jim Forest, *Love Is the Measure: A Biography of Dorothy Day* (New York: Paulist Press, 1986) 56. David E. Shi, *Matthew Josephson: Bourgeois Bohemian* (New Haven: Yale University Press, 1981) 123.

105. Dorothy Day, *The Long Loneliness* (San Francisco: Harper and Row, 1981) 113-114.

106. Caroline Gordon, letter to Sally Wood, 1925, *The Southern Mandarins: Letters of Caroline Gordon to Sally Wood, 1924–1937*, ed. Sally Wood (Baton Rouge: Louisiana State University Press, 1984) 17. Malcolm Cowley, *Exile's Return* 69. Cf. Ann Waldron, *Close Connections: Caroline Gordon and the Southern Renaissance* (New York: G. P. Putnam's Sons, 1987) 41-42, 44-45, 49, 58.

107. William D. Miller, *Dorothy Day: A Biography* (San Francisco: Harper and Row, 1982) 285-288.

108. Nancy Roberts, *Dorothy Day and the "Catholic Worker"* (Albany: State University of New York Press, 1984) 23.

109. Cf. Ann Waldron, *Close Connections* 333. See also Brainard Cheney, "Caroline Gordon's *The Malefactors*," *Sewanee Review* 79 (1971): 360-372.

110. Allen Tate, letter to Donald Davidson, 23 February 1936, *The Literary Correspondence of Donald Davidson and Allen Tate* 297. Cf. Veronica A. Makowsky, *Caroline Gordon: A Biography* (New York: Oxford University Press, 1989) 132-133, 198-199.

111. Minutes of the Convention of the Committee for the Alliance of Agrarian and Distributist Groups in Nashville, Tennessee, 4-5 June 1936. Andrew Nelson Lytle Papers, Vanderbilt University.

4. Philosophy for a Christian Humanism

1. G. K. Chesterton, *Christendom in Dublin* (London: Sheed and Ward, 1933) 78.

2. Ronald Knox, *The Belief of Catholics* 158.

3. Allen Tate, letter to Francis X. Connolly, 16 March 1941. Princeton University Libraries.

4. Ronald Knox, *The Belief of Catholics* 38.

5. C. S. Lewis, *Surprised by Joy* 191, cf. 223, 226.

6. Cf. Appendix E, "Rural Life and the Teachings of St. Thomas Aquinas" in Raymond Phillip Witte, *Twenty-Five Years of Crusading* 243-254.

7. Michael Derrick quoted in Jay P. Corrin, *G. K. Chesterton and Hilaire Belloc* 160.

8. G. K. Chesterton, *Saint Thomas Aquinas: "The Dumb Ox"* (New York: Image Books, 1956) 189.

9. William Halsey, *The Survival of American Innocence* 159.

10. Arnold Sparr, *To Promote, Defend, and Redeem* xiii, 40.

11. Patrick W. Carey, "American Catholic Religious Thought: An Historical Review," *U.S. Catholic Historian* 4 (1985): 138.

12. Gerald McCool, *The Neo-Thomists* (Milwaukee: Marquette University Press, 1994) 2.

13. Cf. Gerald A. McCool, *Catholic Theology in the Nineteenth Century: The Quest for a Unitary Method* (New York: Seabury Press, 1977). See also Maurice de Wulf, *Scholasticism Old and New: An Introduction to Scholastic Philosophy Medieval and Modern*, trans. P. Coffey (Dublin: M. H. Gill and Son, 1907).

14. Yves Congar, *A History of Theology*, trans. and ed. Hunter Guthrie (Garden City, NY: Doubleday, 1968) 185.

15. Leo XIII, *Aeterni patris, The Papal Encyclicals 1878–1903* 26.

16. Mark Schoof, *A Survey of Catholic Theology 1800–1970*, trans. N. D. Smith (Paramus, NJ: Paulist Newman Press, 1970) 151.

17. Pius X, *Pascendi dominici gregis, The Papal Encyclicals 1903–1939* 92.

18. Zsolt Aradi, *Pius XI: The Pope and the Man* (Garden City, NY: Hanover House, 1958) 195.

19. Pius XII, *Humani generis, The Papal Encyclicals 1939–1958*, ed. Claudia Carlen (Raleigh, NC: McGrath, 1981) 180.

20. Yves Congar, *A History of Theology* 187.

21. Maurice de Wulf, "Neo-Scholasticism," *The Catholic Encyclopedia*, 15 vols. (New York: Gilmary Society, 1913) 10: 746.

22. David Tracy, *Blessed Rage for Order* (San Francisco: Harper and Row, 1988) 30.

23. Etienne Gilson, *Letters of Etienne Gilson to Henri de Lubac*, trans. Mary Emily Hamilton (San Francisco: Ignatius Press, 1988) 217. Cf. Gerald A. McCool, *From Unity to Pluralism: The Internal Evolution of Thomism* (New York: Fordham University Press, 1989).

24. George Huntston Williams, *The Mind of John Paul II: Origins of His Thought and Action* (New York: Seabury Press, 1981) 93-103.

25. G. K. Chesterton, *Saint Thomas Aquinas* 23.

26. Jacques Maritain, *The Angelic Doctor*, trans. J. F. Scanlan (New York: Dial Press, 1931) 97, 107.

27. Raissa Maritain, *We Have Been Friends Together and Adventures in Grace*, trans. Julie Kernan (Garden City, NY: Image Books, 1961) 342.

28. G. K. Chesterton, *Saint Thomas Aquinas* 189. Etienne Gilson, *The Spirit of Thomism* (New York: Harper and Row, 1964) 84-102.

29. Raissa Maritain, *We Have Been Friends Together and Adventures in Grace* 352.

30. Quoted in Raissa Maritain, *We Have Been Friends Together and Adventures in Grace* 156.

31. Walter Sullivan, *Allen Tate: A Recollection* 70.

32. Cf. Richard Foster, *The New Romantics: A Reappraisal of the New Criticism* (Bloomington: Indiana University Press, 1962) 120.

33. Allen Tate, lecture, Assumption University, 1958. Princeton University Libraries.

34. Allen Tate, "Religion and the Intellectuals," *Partisan Review* 17 (March 1950): 252.

35. John Henry Newman, *Apologia Pro Vita Sua* 81.

36. Cf. Ann Hulbert, *The Interior Castle: The Art and Life of Jean Stafford* (New York: Alfred A. Knopf, 1992) 109-175. William Doreski, *The Years of Our Friendship: Robert Lowell and Allen Tate* (Jackson: University Press of Mississippi, 1990).

37. John Crowe Ransom, letter to Robert Lowell, 27 April 1943, *Selected Letters of John Crowe Ransom* 307.

38. Ann Waldron, *Close Connections* 257-261.

39. Gerald A. McCool, "Twentieth Century Scholasticism," *Journal of Religion* (1978 Supplement): S209-215.

40. Allen Tate, letter to John M. Dunaway, 4 May 1976, *Exiles and Fugitives* 9.

41. Cf. John M. Dunaway, "Exiles and Fugitives: The Maritain-Tate-Gordon Letters," *From Twilight to Dawn: The Cultural Vision of Jacques Maritain*, ed. Peter A. Redpath (Notre Dame, IN: American Maritain Association and University of Notre Dame, 1990) 27-35.

42. Jacques Maritain, *Creative Intuition in Art and Poetry* (Princeton: Princeton University Press, 1981) 56, 116n, 194n, 201, 233n, 261, 283, 306n, 342, 383, 391, 393, 398n. Cf. Jacques Maritain, *Reflections on America* (New York: Charles Scribner's Sons, 1958) 42. See also Judith Suther, *Raissa Maritain: Pilgrim, Poet, Exile* (New York: Fordham University Press, 1990).

43. Allen Tate, *Collected Poems 1919–1976* 211-214.

44. Russell Kirk, *Eliot and His Age* (Peru, IL: Sherwood Sugden, 1988) 180.

45. Allen Tate, *Essays of Four Decades* 54.

46. Cf. Jacques Maritain, "Poetry and Religion," trans. F. S. Flint, *Criterion* 5 (January 1927): 7-22 and (May 1927): 214-230. Martin C.

D'Arcy, "The Thomistic Synthesis and Intelligence," *Criterion* 6 (September 1927): 210-228.

47. Allen Tate, *Essays of Four Decades* 55.

48. Allen Tate, letter to Jacques Maritain, 13 April 1944, *Exiles and Fugitives* 19.

49. Cf. Louise Cowan, *The Southern Critics* (Dallas: University of Dallas Press, 1972).

50. John Crowe Ransom, *Selected Essays of John Crowe Ransom*, ed. Thomas Daniel Young and John Hindle (Baton Rouge: Louisiana State University Press, 1984) 190. John Crowe Ransom, "In Amicitia" 534.

51. John Crowe Ransom, letter to Allen Tate, 17 September 1936, *Selected Letters of John Crowe Ransom* 217.

52. Allen Tate, letter to Andrew Lytle, 23 December 1954, *The Lytle-Tate Letters* 243.

53. Leslie Fiedler, *What Was Literature? Class Culture and Mass Society* (New York: Simon and Schuster, 1982) 70.

54. Cf. Robert Gorham Davis, "The New Criticism and the Democratic Tradition," *American Scholar* 19 (Winter 1949-50): 9-19.

55. Allen Tate, "The New Criticism," *American Scholar* 20 (1950-51): 93.

56. Father Beatus T. Lucey, O.S.B., personal interview, 17 August 1993. Church records, St. Paul Catholic Church, Princeton, New Jersey.

57. Ann Waldron, *Close Connections* 279.

58. Donald Davidson, letter to Allen Tate, 26 January 1951, *The Literary Correspondence of Donald Davidson and Allen Tate* 354.

59. William Lynch, letter to Allen Tate, 3 February 1953. Princeton University Libraries.

60. *Catholic Authors*, ed. Matthew Hoehn (Newark, NJ: St. Mary's Abbey, 1952) 574-576.

61. Katherine Bregy, "Allen Tate—Paradoxical Pilgrim," *Catholic World* 180 (November 1954): 121-125.

62. Sister Bernetta Quinn, letter to Allen Tate, 21 April 1951. Princeton University Libraries.

63. John Crowe Ransom, "In Amicitia" 538, 529, 539.

64. Harold G. Gardiner, S.J., letter to Allen Tate, 10 February 1954. Terence Y. Mullins, letter to Allen Tate, 15 December 1966. Thomas Francis Ritt, letter to Allen Tate, 25 October 1951. John Alvis, letter to Allen Tate, no date. Richard J. Walsh, letter to Allen Tate, 11 July 1958. Princeton University Libraries.

65. F. E. Flynn, letter to Allen Tate, 25 July 1952. Princeton University Libraries.

66. Frederick G. Hochwalt, letter to Allen Tate, 21 April 1953. J. Stanley Murphy, C.S.B., letters to Allen Tate, 23 June 1958 and 7 July 1958. Princeton University Libraries.

67. Allen Tate, letter to Caroline Gordon, 15 January 1956. Princeton University Libraries.

68. Photograph of Allen Tate by Stephen Spender, September 1952. Princeton University Libraries.

69. Cf. Francis J. Sheed, *The Church and I* (Garden City, NY: Doubleday, 1974) 181.

70. Allen Tate, letter to Caroline Gordon, 30 August 1952. Princeton University Libraries.

71. Cf. Raissa Maritain, *Raissa's Journal*, ed. Jacques Maritain (Albany, NY: Magi Books, 1974) 158-159, 176-177. See also Ralph McInerny, *Art and Prudence* (Notre Dame, IN: University of Notre Dame Press, 1988) 5-6.

72. Cf. Allen Tate, letter to Jacques Maritain, 2 March 1952, *Exiles and Fugitives* 41-43.

73. Allen Tate, letter to Walter J. Ong, 11 April 1953.

74. Allen Tate, "A Symposium: The Agrarians Today," *Shenandoah* 3 (Summer 1952): 29.

75. Allen Tate, letter to Robert Fitzgerald, 1 March 1952, *Exiles and Fugitives* 102.

76. Gale H. Carrithers, Jr., *Mumford, Tate, Eiseley: Watchers in the Night* (Baton Rouge: Louisiana State University Press, 1991) 140.

77. Cf. Radcliffe Squires, "Allen Tate's Terzinas," *Allen Tate and His Work: Critical Evaluations*, ed. Radcliffe Squires (Minneapolis: University of Minnesota, 1972) 291-306. Robert H. Brinkmeyer, *Three Catholic Writers of the Modern South* (Jackson: University Press of Mississippi, 1985) 3-172. Robert Dupree, *Allen Tate and the Augustinian Imagination*.

78. Paul Giles, *American Catholic Arts and Fictions: Culture, Ideology, Aesthetics* (New York: Cambridge University Press, 1992) 209, 204.

79. Allen Tate, *Essays of Four Decades* 447-461.

80. Etienne Gilson, *The Spirit of Mediaeval Philosophy* (Notre Dame, IN: University of Notre Dame Press, 1991) 99.

81. Allen Tate, *The Fathers* (New York: G. P. Putnam's Sons, 1938) 218.

82. Allen Tate, *The Forlorn Demon* (Chicago: Regnery, 1953) 77.

83. Cleanth Brooks, "The Formalist Critic," *Kenyon Review* 13 (Winter 1951): 72. Italics in original.

84. Erich Auerbach, *Mimesis: The Representation of Reality in Western Literature*, trans. Willard R. Trask (Princeton: Princeton University Press, 1974).

85. John Crowe Ransom, *The World's Body* (Baton Rouge: Louisiana State University Press, 1968). Cf. Thomas Aquinas, *Summa theologica* 1.46.1.4.

86. Allen Tate, *Essays of Four Decades* 460.

87. Allen Tate, *Essays of Four Decades* 284.

88. Jacques Maritain, *Three Reformers* 79.

89. Flannery O'Connor, *Mystery and Manners*, ed. Sally and Robert Fitzgerald (New York: Farrar, Straus and Giroux, 1989) 161, 159.

90. Allen Tate, *The Forlorn Demon* 4.

91. Cf. William C. Havard and Walter Sullivan, eds., *A Band of Prophets: The Vanderbilt Agrarians After Fifty Years* (Baton Rouge: Louisiana State University Press, 1982). Thomas Daniel Young, *Waking Their Neighbors Up: The Nashville Agrarians Rediscovered* (Athens: University of Georgia, 1982). Paul A. Bove, "Agriculture and Academe: America's Southern Question," *Boundary 2* 14 (Spring 1986): 169-195. Gale H. Carrithers, Jr., *Mumford, Tate, Eiseley.*

92. Allen Tate, *Mere Literature and the Lost Traveller* n.p.

93. T. S. Eliot, *After Strange Gods* 66.

94. Mary McCarthy quoted in Carol Brightmen, *Writing Dangerously: Mary McCarthy and Her World* (New York: Clarkson Potter, 1992) 156.

95. H. Richard Niebuhr, *Christ and Culture* (New York: Harper and Row, 1975) 45-82.

96. T. S. Eliot, "The Metaphysical Poets," *Selected Prose of T. S. Eliot*, ed. Frank Kermode (New York: Harcourt Brace Jovanovich/Farrar, Straus and Giroux, 1975) 64.

97. Quoted in *The Spirituality of the American Transcendentalists*, ed. Catherine L. Albanese (Macon, GA: Mercer University Press, 1988) 1.

98. Allen Tate, *Essays of Four Decades* 284.

99. Allen Tate, *Reason in Madness* 61.

100. Allen Tate, "The Revolt Against Literature," *New Republic* 49 (9 February 1927): 330.

101. John Dewey, *A Common Faith* (New Haven: Yale University Press, 1962) 9.

102. Philip J. Lee, *Against the Protestant Gnostics* (New York: Oxford University Press, 1987) 176-185.

103. Quentin Anderson, *The Imperial Self: An Essay in American Literary and Cultural History* (New York: Alfred A. Knopf, 1971) 3.

104. Allen Tate, "Confusion and Poetry," *Sewanee Review* 38 (April-June 1930): 137. Cf. Alfred North Whitehead, *Religion in the Making* (New York: Meridian, 1974) 16.

105. Cf. J. David Hoeveler, Jr., *The New Humanism: A Critique of Modern America, 1900–1940* (Charlottesville: University Press of Virginia, 1977).

106. Irving Babbitt, *Representative Writings*, ed. George A. Panichas (Lincoln: University of Nebraska Press, 1981) 13.

107. Allen Tate, "Tiresias," *Nation* 123 (17 November 1926): 509.

108. Allen Tate, "The Same Fallacy of Humanism," *Bookman* 71 (March 1930): 36.

109. Allen Tate, *Memoirs and Opinions* 190.

110. "Introduction: A Statement of Principles," *I'll Take My Stand* xliv.

111. Allen Tate, "Remarks on the Southern Religion," *I'll Take My Stand* 156.

112. Allen Tate, "Religion and the Intellectuals" 251, 253.

113. Allen Tate, letter to Donald Davidson, 27 October 1951, *The Literary Correspondence of Donald Davidson and Allen Tate* 355.

114. Thomas Aquinas, *Summa theologica* 1.13.5. Karl Adam, *The Spirit of Catholicism*, trans. Justin McCann, rev. ed. (New York: Macmillan, 1946) 177.

115. Allen Tate, *Essays of Four Decades* 592.

116. John M. Dunaway, introduction, *Exiles and Fugitives* 2.

117. Michael Millgate, "An Interview with Allen Tate," *Shenandoah* 12 (Spring 1961): 31.

118. James Hitchcock, *The New Enthusiasts and What They Are Doing to the Catholic Church* (Chicago: Thomas More Press, 1982) 104.

119. Allen Tate, letter, *New York Times* 1 February 1951: 24.

120. Allen Tate, "Orthodoxy and the Standard of Literature," *New Republic* 128 (5 January 1953): 24.

121. John Henry Newman, *The Idea of a University*, ed. Martin J. Svaglic (New York: Holt, Rinehart and Winston, 1964) 174. Cf. Flannery O'Connor, letter to Sally and Robert Fitzgerald, undated, Summer 1953, *The Habit of Being*, ed. Sally Fitzgerald (New York: Farrar, Straus, Giroux, 1979) 60.

122. Allen Tate, "Orthodoxy and the Standard of Literature" 24.

123. Allen Tate, lecture, Assumption University, 1958. Princeton University Libraries.

124. Cf. Bernard J. F. Lonergan, *Method in Theology* (Toronto: University of Toronto Press, 1990) 73. See also Ralph McInerny, *Art and Prudence* 137-173.

125. Michael Millgate, "An Interview with Allen Tate" 31.

126. Allen Tate, *The Forlorn Demon* 41, 36, 38. Cf. H. Richard Niebuhr, *Christ and Culture* 116-148.

127. Malcolm Ross, rev. of *The Forlorn Demon*, by Allen Tate, *Thought* 29 (Summer 1952): 301.

128. Patrick W. Carey, *The Roman Catholics* (Westport, CT: Greenwood Press, 1993) 93-114.

129. Allen Tate, "Significance of the Convention." Princeton University Libraries.

130. Allen Tate, "Christ and the Unicorn," *Sewanee Review* 63 (1955): 178-179, 181.

131. G. K. Chesterton, *Saint Thomas Aquinas* 119.

132. Allen Tate, letter to Andrew Lytle, 23 December 1954, *The Lytle-Tate Letters* 243.

133. Gale H. Carrithers, Jr., *Mumford, Tate, Eiseley* 150. Lewis P. Simpson, "The Southern Republic of Letters and *I'll Take My Stand*," *A Band of Prophets: The Vanderbilt Agrarians After Fifty Years* 91.

134. Quoted in Radcliffe Squires, *Allen Tate: A Literary Biography* 189.

135. Allen Tate, "Orthodoxy and the Standard of Literature" 24.

136. Allen Tate, *Reason in Madness* 19.

137. Thomas J. J. Altizer, "The Atheistic Ground of America," *Anglican Theological Review* 71 (Summer 1989): 264.

138. Allen Tate, *The Forlorn Demon* 8, 14 and *Essays of Four Decades* 523.

5. Traveler Lost in a Forest

1. William James, *The Varieties of Religious Experience* 238.

2. George Santayana, letter to Cyril Clemens, December 1947 in *Commonweal* 57 (24 October 1952): 61.

3. Allen Tate, *Mere Literature and the Lost Traveller* n.p.

4. Daniel Joseph Singal, *The War Within* 232-260.

5. Allen Tate, "Gentleman in a Dustcoat," *Sewanee Review* 76 (Summer 1968): 378.

6. Walter Sullivan, *Allen Tate: A Recollection* 48.

7. Julian Green, *The Apprentice Writer* (New York: Marion Boyars, 1993) 115.

8. Flannery O'Connor, letter to "A," 4 April 1958, *The Habit of Being* 275.

9. Georgina Pell Curtis, ed., *Beyond the Road to Rome* (St. Louis: Herder, 1914) 65.

10. Cf. James Hennessey, *American Catholics* 307-331.

11. Robert Penn Warren, *All the King's Men* (San Diego: Harcourt Brace Jovanovich, 1974) 438.

12. John A. O'Brien edited three volumes of brief autobiographical

conversion narratives typical of the Catholic Revival: *The Road to Damascus: The Spiritual Pilgrimage of Fifteen Converts to Catholicism* (Garden City, NY: Doubleday, 1949); *The Way to Emmaus: The Intimate Personal Stories of Converts to the Catholic Faith* (New York: McGraw-Hill, 1953); *Roads to Rome: The Intimate Personal Stories of Converts to the Catholic Faith* (New York: Macmillan, 1954).

13. Evelyn Waugh, "Come Inside," *The Road to Damascus* 18.

14. G. K. Chesterton, *The Catholic Church and Conversion* (New York: Macmillan, 1927) 93.

15. John Henry Newman, *Apologia Pro Vita Sua* 184.

16. L. Sullivan Ives, *The Trials of a Mind in its Progress to Catholicism* (Boston: Patrick Donahoe, 1854) 233.

17. William James, *The Varieties of Religious Experience* 189.

18. John Henry Newman, *Loss and Gain: The Story of a Convert* (London: Burns and Oates, 1886) 16ff.

19. Peter L. Berger, *A Far Glory: The Quest for Faith in an Age of Credulity* (New York: Anchor Books, 1992) 169-190.

20. Richard Foster, *The New Romantics* 129.

21. Philip Gleason, "In Search of Unity: American Catholic Thought 1920–1960," *Catholic Historical Review* 65 (April 1979): 185.

22. Cf. Lawrence S. Cunningham, *The Catholic Heritage* (New York: Crossroad, 1993) 147-166.

23. Allen Tate, letter to Francis X. Connolly, 16 March 1941. Princeton University Libraries.

24. Allen Tate, letter to Thomas Francis Ritt, 12 November 1951. Quoted in Radcliffe Squires, *Allen Tate: A Literary Biography* 189.

25. Vincent F. Blehl, "Liberalism in Current Criticism," *America* 86 (1 March 1952): 589.

26. Allen Tate, letter to Caroline Gordon, 14 October 1957. Princeton University Libraries.

27. William Lynch, letter to Allen Tate, no date. Princeton University Libraries.

28. Harry Sylvester, "Problems of the Catholic Writer," *Atlantic Monthly* 181 (January 1948): 109-113.

29. Richard Hofstadter, *Anti-Intellectualism in American Life* (New York: Vintage Books, 1963) 140.

30. Allen Tate, letter to Caroline Gordon, 24 January 1956. Princeton University Libraries.

31. Allen Tate, letters to Caroline Gordon, no date, 8 March 1958. Cf. Allen Tate, address to psychiatric association, Washington, DC, 1957. Princeton University Libraries.

32. Allen Tate, letters to Caroline Gordon, 19 August 1958, 15

January 1957, 9 April 1957, 2 January 1955. Princeton University Libraries.

33. Allen Tate, letters to Caroline Gordon, 21 January 1956, 13 February 1962, 1 February 1964. Princeton University Libraries.

34. Allen Tate, letter to Andrew Lytle, 10 August 1959, *The Lytle-Tate Letters* 281. Allen Tate, letter to Caroline Gordon, 18 January 1963. Princeton University Libraries.

35. William Lynch, letter to Allen Tate, 18 November [no year]. Princeton University Libraries.

36. Arnold Sparr, *To Promote, Defend, and Redeem* 163-170.

37. John Pick, "The New Criticism," *Renascence* 3 (Spring 1951): 106.

38. Cf. Donald Attwater, "The Decline of Distributism," *Commonweal* 53 (2 February 1951): 421-422.

39. Cf. Robert Wuthnow, *The Restructuring of American Religion: Society and Faith Since World War II* (Princeton: Princeton University Press, 1988).

40. John O'Malley, *Tradition and Transition: Historical Perspectives on Vatican II* (Wilmington, DE: Michael Glazier, 1989) 17.

41. Cf. Joseph Scheuer, *The De-Romanization of the American Catholic Church* (New York: Macmillan, 1966).

42. Gabriel Daly, "Catholicism and Modernity," *Journal of the American Academy of Religion* 53 (1985): 782.

43. Karl Rahner, "Towards a Fundamental Theological Interpretation of Vatican II," *Vatican II: The Unfinished Agenda*, ed. Lucian Richard et al. (New York: Paulist Press, 1987) 9-32.

44. Vincent A. Yzermans, *A New Pentecost: Vatican Council II: Session 1* (Westminster, MD: Newman Press, 1963). George A. Lindbeck, *The Future of Roman Catholic Theology: Vatican II–Catalyst for Change* (Philadelphia: Fortress Press, 1962).

45. Quoted in James Hitchcock, *The Decline and Fall of Radical Catholicism* (New York: Herder and Herder, 1971) 211.

46. Fulton J. Sheen, *Treasure in Clay: The Autobiography of Fulton J. Sheen* (Garden City, NY: Doubleday, 1980) 247-248.

47. *Letters of Etienne Gilson to Henri de Lubac* 128-129.

48. Jacques Maritain, *The Peasant of the Garonne: An Old Layman Questions Himself about the Present Time*, trans. Michael Cuddihy and Elizabeth Hughes (New York: Holt, Rinehart and Winston, 1968).

49. Cf. William D. Dinges and James Hitchcock, "Roman Catholic Traditionalism and Activist Conservatism in the United States," *Fundamentalisms Observed*, ed. Martin E. Marty and R. Scott Appleby (Chicago: University of Chicago Press, 1991) 66-141. See also Daniele Menozzi, "Opposition to the Council (1966–84)," *The Reception of*

Vatican II, ed. Giuseppe Alberigo, Jean-Pierre Jossua, and Joseph A. Komonchak, trans. Matthew J. O'Connell (Washington, DC: Catholic University of America, 1987) 325-348.

50. Malachi Martin, *The Decline and Fall of the Roman Church* (New York: G. P. Putnam's Sons, 1981) 272.

51. Frans Jozef van Beeck, *Catholic Identity After Vatican II: Three Types of Faith in One Church* (Chicago: Loyola University Press, 1985).

52. George A. Lindbeck, *The Nature of Doctrine: Religion and Theology in a Postliberal Age* (Philadelphia: Westminster Press, 1984).

53. H. Stuart Hughes, *Sophisticated Rebels: The Political Culture of European Dissent 1968-1987* (Cambridge, MA: Harvard University Press, 1988) 72.

54. Cf. James Hitchcock, "Postmortem on a Rebirth" 224.

55. James Terence Fisher, *The Catholic Counterculture in America* 250.

56. Debra Campbell, "The Laity in the Age of Aggiornamento, 1960-1969," *Transforming Parish Ministry* 253-266. Cf. Joseph Saski, "The Lay Apostolate of the Modern Time," *The Lay Apostolate and the Hierarchy* (Ottowa: University of Ottowa Press, 1967) 73-102.

57. Russell Jacoby, *The Last Intellectuals: American Culture in the Age of Academe* (New York: Basic Books, 1987).

58. Philip Gleason, "In Search of Unity: American Catholic Thought 1920-1960" 188.

59. James J. Bacik, *Contemporary Theologians* (New York: Triumph Books, 1989) 232.

60. Francis J. Sheed, *The Church and I* 103.

61. Cf. Philip Gleason, *Keeping the Faith* 202-225.

62. Jacques Maritain, *The Peasant of the Garonne* 13.

63. James Hitchcock, *The Recovery of the Sacred* (New York: Seabury Press, 1974) 55.

64. Etienne Gilson, letter to Henri de Lubac, 22 July 1965, *Letters of Etienne Gilson to Henri de Lubac* 128. Walter Sullivan, *Allen Tate: A Recollection* 51.

65. Allen Tate, letters to Caroline Gordon, 18 January 1958, 12 November 1963. Princeton University Libraries.

66. James Terence Fisher, *The Catholic Counterculture in America* 1-69.

67. Quoted in Lawrence Cunningham, *The Catholic Heritage* 143.

68. Mark Noll speaks of Walker Percy and Flannery O'Connor as "alienated losers twice over—as Southerners in a culture dominated by Northern industriousness and as Catholics in an overwhelmingly Protestant South." *A History of Christianity in the United States and Canada* (Grand Rapids, MI: Eerdmans, 1992) 418.

69. Walter Sullivan, *Allen Tate: A Recollection* 59.

70. Joseph Schwartz, letter to author, 26 October 1992.

71. Cf. Allen Tate, "A Humanist Looks at the Humanities," tape recording, University of Minnesota.

72. Allen Tate, *Mere Literature and the Lost Traveller* n.p.

73. Karl Adam, *The Spirit of Catholicism* 6, 110.

74. Katherine Anne Porter, letter to John Malcolm Brinnin, 2 May 1956, *Letters of Katherine Anne Porter*, ed. Isabel Bayley (New York: Atlantic Monthly Press, 1990) 505.

75. Graham Greene, letter to Alberto Huerta, August 1989, Alberto Huerta, "Graham, We Hardly Knew Ye," *Commonweal* (14 July 1995): 22.

76. Allen Tate, *Essays of Four Decades* 357.

77. Elizabeth Sarcone, "Andrew Lytle: A Modern Traditionalist," *The Vanderbilt Tradition: Essays in Honor of Thomas Daniel Young*, ed. Mark Royden Winchell (Baton Rouge: Louisiana State University Press, 1991) 155.

78. Allen Tate, "Religion and the Intellectuals" 250.

Index

52–55, 63, 65, 67, 68, 80, 83,
90, 103, 111
Benedict XV, Pope, 28
Berdyaev, Nicholas, 65
Berger, Peter, 104
Bergson, Henri, 14, 47
Berman, Marshall, 44
Bernanos, George, 13, 21
Bishop, Howard, 59, 62
Bishop, John Peale, 66
Blake, William, 116
Blehl, Vincent, 106
Bloom, Harold, 5, 17
Bloy, Léon, 13, 47
Bonaventure, St., 74
Bookman (magazine), 65, 80
Borden, Lucille Papen, 17
Borsodi, Ralph, 57, 59
Boston College, 84, 96
Bourke, Vernon, 84
Bregy, Katherine, 102
Brinkmeyer, Robert, 86
Brooks, Cleanth, 68, 81, 88
Brooks, Van Wyck, 16
Brownson, Orestes, 15, 26
Bryan, William Jennings, 33
"Buried Lake, The" (Tate), 86–87
Burns, Gene, 6, 52

Campbell, Debra, 114
Carey, Patrick, 73, 97
Carrithers, Gale, 86, 98
Casey, Marion, 83
Catholic Action, 20, 52, 114
Catholic Action (magazine), 60
Catholic Authors, 83
Catholic Book Club, 19
Catholic Education Association,
84
Catholic Encyclopedia, 76
Catholic Evidence Guild, 20, 79

Catholic Land movement. *See*
Distributism
Catholic Literary Revival, 4,
11ff., 105–7, 109ff., 117–18
Catholic Literary Revival, The
(Alexander), 15, 29–30
Catholic Poetry Society, 19, 83,
105
Catholic Renascence Society, 19,
109
Catholic Rural Life (magazine), 59
Catholic Rural Life Bureau, 59
Catholic Worker (newspaper), 60,
70–71
Catholic Workers, 60–61, 70–71,
79
Catholic World (magazine), 83
Chapman, Charles C., 68
Chardin, Pierre Teilhard de, 113,
115
Chesterton, G. K., 13, 14, 15, 21,
27, 28, 30, 50, 52–55, 64–66,
72, 73, 80, 98, 103, 111, 117
"Christ and the Unicorn" (Tate),
98
Cincinnati Conservatory of
Music, 32
Civil War, 45–47
Civiltà cattolica (magazine), 74
Claudel, Paul, 13, 14
Cobbett, William, 55
College of St. Thomas, 84
Collins, Seward, 65, 66, 68, 80
Committee of Catholics for
Cultural Action, 86
Commonweal (magazine), 12, 16,
19, 60, 111
Confessions (Augustine), 102
"Confusion and Poetry" (Tate),
78
Congar, Yves, 74, 114

ISAAC HECKER STUDIES
IN RELIGION AND AMERICAN CULTURE

Other Books in the Series